SEEING

When Art and Faith Intersect

Douglas G. Campbell

University Press of America,® Inc.
Lanham · New York · Oxford

♾™ The paper used in this publication meets the minimum
requirements of American National Standard for Information
Sciences—Permanence of Paper for Printed Library Materials,
ANSI Z39.48—1984

To my wife and best friend Rebecca Propst

CONTENTS

LIST OF ILLUSTRATIONS

PREFACE

Seeing is primarily the result of a 1997-98 Sabbatical, granted by George Fox University. Three of the essays, "Seeing," "Words," and Being," were the basis for "Seeing and Believing: Art as A Pathway to Knowing," as the 1999 Spring Faculty lecture given at George Fox University. These brief essays are my attempt to address significant issues faced by contemporary artists and Christians as they think about and interact with art.

I appreciate the help of many people for their help with this book. George Fox University provided a sabbatical, which gave me an opportunity to research and begin writing. The librarians at George Fox University graciously introduced me to new on-line sources; they also processed many requests for books and articles. Jo Lewis, Ed.D. edited this manuscript. Jo Lewis, Ed.D., William Jolliff, Ph.D. and Mark McLeod, Ph.D. read and gave helpful insights on specific chapters. Bruce Arnold provided computer support. I also thank the art majors in my Spring 2000, Art and Christ class at George Fox University for their comments and input.

I acknowledge the editors of University Press of America for their assistance in bringing this book to print. However, most of all, I wish to thank my wife, L. Rebecca Propst, Ph.D., for reading and re-reading each chapter numerous times and for her support over several years in bringing this book to print. I also thank my sons Joshua and Ian for their forbearance, as they allowed me to work when they might rather have had me present with them for an alternative activity.

Most Biblical citations are from the New Revised Standard Version of the Bible. Those that are not are indicated.

All faults and errors are mine alone.

Douglas G. Campbell, *Day One, Dance of Darkness and Light*, acrylics
on canvas, 54"x40", 1996

Introduction

Dance of Darkness and Light

> And God said, "Let there be light"; and there was light. And God saw
> that the light was good; and God separated the light from the darkness.
> God called the light Day, and the darkness he called Night. And there
> was evening and there was morning, one day.
>
> Gn 1:3-5, RSV

Christians believe that from the very beginning humans have existed
in a world with both darkness and light, because God made it so. We
may see because of this light that God made. However, even though
God made light, and called it good, God did not destroy the darkness,
this darkness which hinders seeing. Although darkness hinders seeing,
it also draws our attention to light. It is one source of light that this
book is about.

Seeing is about seeing and believing in God. Art by Christians has
experienced a renewal in the past several decades. Artists of faith now
enthusiastically create artworks expressive of Christian spirituality.
These brief essays focus on various issues that may concern artists of
faith, issues such as Postmodernism, demons, quality, authenticity and
individualism.

The essays are not intended to bring closure to any of the topics
they introduce. To the contrary, they are intended as starting places.
Through discussion of these topics I hope to encourage artists, and
those for whom these artists make their artworks, so that this darkness
may be illuminated.

Such illumination is needed, for artists of faith found little
encouragement within the Modernism that dominated the twentieth
century, the Modernism that encouraged artists to focus on form alone,
on limiting content to form alone. This left no room, at least within
the mainstream, for art to image forth a transcendent God. With the
questioning of Modernism that occurred in the second half of the

twentieth century, artists of faith could begin to find contemporary ways to express their ideas, thoughts and beliefs.

It would be dishonest of me to allow you to believe that I am in any way a disinterested and objective observer of the type of art under discussion.   As a Christian who teaches at a Quaker university and belongs to a Mennonite Church, I am biased in favor of the Christian faith.   In spite of my current attachment to two Christian bodies not noted for the strength of their visual art traditions, I am an advocate of visual art, including art that involves itself with Christian imagery, subjects or content.   My eclectic Christian background has been formed through my direct connection with Methodist, Presbyterian, Wesleyan, Episcopalian and Mennonite churches.   In addition, many indirect connections that inform my thinking come from a variety of other Christian sources.

I am also strongly biased in favor of finding value in the visual arts. For my undergraduate degree and one graduate degree I specialized in the studio disciplines of printmaking, painting and photography.   I have worked and continue to work with a variety of media—relief printing, etching, painting, drawing and mixed media.   A large portion of my own artwork is involved directly with the use of Christian imagery, subjects or content.   As a result of this I have been thinking about the relationship between the visual arts and Christianity from the point of view of the artist, or from the point of an arts historian, or from the point of view of a teacher of both art history and studio art.

As I alternate among these areas, I have found only a very small amount of information and writing available on the use of Christian imagery, subjects and content in contemporary art.   For some time an idea, which now in some ways resembles what is here collected, began to grow inside me.   A sabbatical from George Fox University provided me with an opportunity for fashioning that idea and giving it written form.

However, what I have written is not the last word on the subject of contemporary Christian imagery, subjects and content in art.   It is rather a small step, one that I hope leads to further dialogue and more importantly more exposure for the artists who work in this area.

Will Christians and church bodies acknowledge that art and artists can play a significant role within Christian life?   For most Christians, faith and worship and prayer and theological insights are hampered by the lack of significant visual stimulation and input.   If this book, in some small way, brings about a greater acceptance of the value of art for Christians, then it will have been worth the time and effort.

These essays are intended to resemble an art exhibit. In many art exhibits there is no set path to follow. If someone blocks our view, we go on to another work and then return to look at the artwork unimpeded. Readers may follow their own path; they need not feel obliged to read these essays in the order presented.

Essay 1

Postmodernism

> Postmodern scholarship, to its credit, attempts to restore art to its external references. Believing that texts have no meaning apart from their *con*text, postmodern critics reject the idea that the work of art is some isolated, privileged object. Instead, they emphasize the work's relationships to society, nature, and human life. Relating art to the rest of reality is promising, opening up possibilities for art that fully engages moral and spiritual issues. Postmodern aesthetic theories can in many ways vindicate Christian artists and Christian critics.[1]
>
> Gene Edward Veith, Jr.

Postmodern thought has lead to a reevaluation of the ways we approach thinking about the past and the artifacts produced in the past. It aims for a more egalitarian approach to viewing the past and its effect upon the present. This contrasts with the Modernists' view of the Modern world, a world towards which all of the historical past had been directed. At the same time, Modernism entailed the rejection of that very past that had given it birth. Instead faith was placed in rationalism, technological innovation, advanced psychological thinking, scientific discovery and artistic innovation.

Above all the Modernist world-view depended upon belief in a narrative view of progress. For the visual artist this meant at least two things. Artists must move forward using a process involving innovative experimentation which was built upon the foundation of artistic advances of the previous generation of artists. At the same time they could only be consistent, as they progressed towards the future, if they rejected the very past upon which they had built.

Secondly, Modern artists came to believe that artistic progress is achieved only by narrowing the focus of art.   Anyone who could not support the Modernist mindset was either reviled as a philistine or ignored as backward, and therefore irrelevant.   Modernism, in spite of the rhetoric of freedom its adherents propagated, depended upon domination by an intellectual elite.

Postmodernism, on the other hand, allows each tradition, each ethnic group, the chance to present (or re-present) its own past and set its own agenda for the future.   This new, perhaps more generous, way of thinking is both positive and negative.

On the positive side Postmodernism tends to question the art historical views of the past.   The historical model that has dominated traditional art history has been the narrative of the mainstream, in which the artistic style of each historical period is seen to be both a reaction to and rooted in what preceded it.   So one might say the Gothic style represents both a partial break with and a partial continuation of Romanesque style.   Styles that did not fit within this mainstream narrative were counted as backwaters or side channels and given less consideration.

With Postmodernism there is no longer one mainstream narrative; instead this model allows for multiple overlapping and interweaving narratives to coexist, though some may be stronger or more robust than others.   Thus when we look at how the past is presented, we are given permission to question how traditional art historians and other writers have modeled and shaped, trimmed and pruned the historical narrative of the mainstream

Because this Postmodernist model encourages multiple narratives, we are allowed to question the art historical fallacy of the "mainstream" that has been the basis of much art historical research and writing. This fallacy depended in the past upon a "survival of the fittest" approach to history, and assumes that one style or conceptual model for art must dominate the artistic arena within each particular time and place.

Thus the job of the art historian was to determine which style was dominant and record the births and deaths of styles and their lineage, much the way one might record the history of a royal family.   One unfortunate aspect of the "mainstream" conceptual approach has been that it has allowed much of the art produced to be ignored and overlooked by historians and tossed onto the trash heap of oblivion. So artists who worked outside the "mainstream" became a-historical beings and not worthy of consideration.

The mainstream approach can be placed at the feet of Hegel, since his view of history relied on the model of thesis, anti-thesis and synthesis, which presupposes a mainstream with one dialog. His model presumes that only two representative voices (the thesis and anti-thesis) can exist at any one time. It assumes that there is only one historical arena (the West) at any one time.

The Hegelian approach required that each viewer wear blinders so that he or she is not distracted from the straight and narrow path. Thus, for example, fifteenth century Florentine art, because it could be seen as a clear antithesis to international style Gothic art, is considered mainstream, indeed paradigmatic for the Italian Renaissance. On the other hand Sienese art, because it is not so clearly antithetical to the Gothic style of art, is considered to be a backwash or eddy rather than the mainstream.

Since art history as a discipline had its birth in the nineteenth century and matured in the twentieth century, it is not surprising that Hegel's historical model had such a powerful influence.

Because this view of history so dominated the Modern world, it is again not surprising that artists themselves have come to believe its veracity. Belief in a mainstream was also encouraged and supported by the new educational model for artistic training. Instead of the old studio system based upon the structure of the medieval guilds, or the model of the independent artist as spiritual genius, what emerged was the academic model. The training of the artist was taken over by the very institutional apparatus that also espoused the idea of the historical "mainstream," academia. And once artists were trained to this model and gained faith in its efficacy, they saw that the only way to achieve historical existence was to participate in and do homage to the "mainstream."

In the twentieth century mainstream art critics like Clement Greenberg (an influential critic of the 1950's and 1960's) wrote: "Content is to be dissolved so completely into form that the work of art or literature cannot be reduced in whole or in part to anything not itself."[2]

Greenberg envisioned such non-referential artistic output as the inevitable next chapter for the mainstream history of art. So he worked to channel artists into the ever-narrower range of possibilities that non-referential art allowed. Inevitably this restricted channel could not contain the power and possibility of art. So Postmodernism with its acceptance of artistic diversity emerged.

How long Postmodernism will remain the accepted view cannot be predicted.   At present, the levees that forced the mainstream to remain within its banks have been breached.   For now at least many channels flow, each following its own course.

So while it lasts, the Postmodernist approach to art history allows us to re-vision the past and the present.   One great value is that it allows voice to many that were denied in the past.   The days of the Hegelian dueling duet (Baroque artists displacing the Renaissance artists or the Post-Impressionists displacing the Impressionists) have been put aside.

This New World of art historical inquiry may often resemble the multitudes of workers babbling at the base of the uncompleted Tower of Babel (the citadel of history), and thus is either disturbing or alarming to the keepers of history.   But even for such keepers the results may be positive.

In this book I am taking advantage of the window of opportunity opened by a Postmodernist approach.   Currently thousands of artists make use of imagery, subjects and/or content that clearly reflects Christian ideas and beliefs.   But prior to the deluge of Postmodernism no "serious" art historian would have considered the study of contemporary Christian art works as a worthwhile task.

"Contemporary Christian" was, to the modern art historian, merely an oxymoron.   In this supposed Post-Christian world, Christian art was neatly confined within the domain of the past.   Specifically, Christian art had had its periods of dominance.   These began with the Early Christian period and ran through Byzantine, Carolingian, Romanesque, Gothic and into the Renaissance, from about 300-1600 C.E.   Christian art of the seventeenth century was reinvigorated by the Counter Reformation.   However in the following century, with the Enlightenment, once faith in reason became the victorious anti-thesis, Christian subjects and content were seen as either marginal or anachronistic remnants of a conquered and defeated voice.

However, now that the "mainstream" itself has been vanquished, Christian voices can again speak with some hope of a hearing. Thus contemporary artworks incorporating Christian imagery, subjects and content and the investigation of contemporary Christian art have become acceptable, if not necessarily respectable.

Any investigation into the use of Christian imagery, subjects and/or content confronts some intriguing and at times frustrating realities within the Postmodern environment.   For not only does Postmodernism allow for many voices to speak, it allows them to speak in any language, native or non-native.   Thus since the subjects, content and/or imagery of Christianity are a part of western culture, they have become the property of anyone who wishes to use them.

One does not need to be a Christian or believe in the validity of Christianity in order to make use of Christian symbols, Christian images or Christian subjects. Artists who make use of them do so from a variety of perspectives and with a variety of objectives.

Postmodernism allows for many voices to speak--but some are more politically correct than others. So some contemporary artists find Christianity to be an anathema. They do so because many that proclaimed themselves to be Christians are seen to be guilty of crimes, evils and horrendous deceits. Other contemporary artists find in Christianity positive values, which they can applaud even though they personally are not adherents. This variety of artistic approach to imagery, subjects and content is not limited to Christianity. With Postmodernism any tradition, any religion, any history, is an environment without fences for artists with either benevolent or predatory instincts.

This fence-less, boundary-free Postmodernist environment has no dominating authority to act as cultural police force or impartial judge. Therefore artists who are Christians and also use Christian imagery, subjects and content will have to contend with adherents of other religious, moral and cultural perspectives. Complications may occur when a multitude of divergent voices clamor to be heard.

The danger is always that that the art of the minority will become lost on this vast sea of images. Even more important is the danger that the artists representing these minorities will lose their very selves.

When many voices are competing for attention, or in the case of visual objects, for the chance to be seen, it may appear as though chaos dominates. Each artist who wants her work to be seen beyond some narrow circle must endeavor to paint or cast or form artworks that will not be overwhelmed by the chaotic babble of the Postmodernist environment. Whether the artwork communicates the "sound of sheer silence" (1 Kgs 19:12) or "flashes forth flames of fire" depends on what is imaged forth. Perhaps sheer silence will gain attention where many voices speak, or fire may give light where darkness keeps us from seeing.

Notes

1. Gene Edward Vieth, Jr., *Postmodern Times: A Christian Guide to Contemporary Thought and Culture* (Wheaton, Illinois: Crossway Books, 1994), 96.

2. Clement Greenberg, *Art and Culture: Critical Essays* (Boston: Beacon Press), 1961.

Essay 2

Truth

Tell the Truth but tell it slant--
Success in Circuit lies
Too bright for our infirm Delight
The Truth's superb surprise
As Lightning to the children eased
With explanation kind
The Truth must dazzle gradually
Or every man be blind—[1]

Emily Dickinson

Truth is an issue that many advocates of Postmodernism would prefer to ignore.   When all styles, all cultures, all ethnic groups, all religious groups, all ideologically-directed groups are given voice, what happens to truth?   We could take a Postmodernist approach to truth as well.   We could say, "There are many truths and all of them are equally valid."   However, no group or individual actually believes this is the case.   Each of us thinks our style of painting, our ideological approach or our religion is better.   If the way we follow were no better than other ways, then why would we persist in following it?   How would any religion survive if its leadership said, "Our Religion A is a fine choice, but Religion R and Religion C are equally good, so why don't you try them out to see whether or not you find them equally appealing?"

Individuals may take a smorgasbord approach to religious affiliation and practice.   But so far as I am aware religious leaders do not.   Similarly, ideological groups do not assert that other ideologies are equal to their own.   I have not heard of Marxists asserting that Capitalist ideology is equally valid, or the reverse.

So how do we go about reconciling the right to speak out and to have a voice, but as we do this, realize that all voices are not necessarily equal? Perhaps the answer is "What I believe is right for me but not for you; each person has the right to believe what he or she chooses to believe." Such a permissive approach sounds workable. For all individuals do choose to believe what seems to fit with their life experiences and circumstances.

It works well until individuals or groups that hold different beliefs come into conflict with one another. It works until belief influences decisions and actions that affect individuals or groups with a diverse set of beliefs. Then the assertion of equality of cultures, religions, styles, ethnicity and ideology begins to unravel. We learn that your beliefs are fine and dandy as long as they don't conflict with my beliefs. Further, it is then, at least functionally, if not intellectually and or spiritually, that we begin to justify our claims with the language of superiority. Our justification usually ends up being linked to truth, not just a truth, but the truth. For at some level, even though a concept of many truths is appealing and seems intellectually responsible and generous in a world filled with diversity, it is not appealing in the arena of politics, international relations or domestic relations.

We do not hold the truths of the opposition party to be sufficient to justify their political claims. We do not hold the truths of neighboring nations to be sufficient to justify another nation's trade policies that hurt us economically. The list is endless. The result is that functionally we believe in a truth, not many truths.

Might we switch from many truths to many ways to truth? If so, can we still maintain a link with Postmodernist vocal empowerment, while we also acknowledge that the coexistence of many truths, even conflicting truths, is intellectually awkward?

So instead of having many truths we have many ways to truth. But is this a solution? It will not take long to discover that asserting that my way to truth is superior to your way to truth is no better functionally than the idea of equality of truths. For when my way to truth comes in conflict with your way to truth, I will claim that my way is better. For if it were not better, then why do I cling to it and not cleave to your way to truth?

Soon it becomes clear that the "ways to truth" path is tenable only so long as our ways to truth do not confront each other. Once they confront, we must decide which one is better and choose; we do not decide that both ways are equally good, because that would lead into a maze of contradictions--we would be forced into walking in two directions at the same time. How do we solve this dilemma?

We solve it by acknowledging that all ways to truth are not equal. Differing ways to truth must still lead to truth, and what is the value of taking a path that leads to part or parts of the truth when another path will lead us more directly to the whole truth? Our difficulty is in deciding which path leads to the whole truth rather than to parts of the truth. Our goal as humans is to struggle with this very issue. Christians believe that through Christ we will be led to the truth. We do not always agree on the details of this journey in Christ towards truth. As humans we haven't the ability to fully discern truth. The best we can do, as finite beings, is to test truth claims.

And the best we can do as artists is share the results of our struggles to find and know truth when we are in its presence. This is not simple. However, some issues are clear at the onset. For example, war is evil and compassion is good. Or, on the other hand, greed is evil and hospitality is good.

Art is one very effective way of communicating these truths. Should we as artists claim to know what truth is in all instances? No, but we cannot help but enter the dialogue. For whenever we make a vase, or drawing, or installation, we speak forth a vision about what is, or was, or could be; and we do it in a way that is evaluation filled, because of the many contextual references we must employ when we transform a concept into fact.

As individual artists we can image pieces of the truth, or ideas about what truth is, or what is true, or celebrations of what is true and declarations of what is false. We will surely step off the path to truth at times. But if through our journey and the artistic mileposts we craft we invite or entice others into searching for truth, then we will have succeeded. Christian artists are not called to be perfect in their search for truth, for God would not expect such perfection among those who acknowledge their own sinfulness. We are called to follow Christ's lead. His life led to pain, it led to service and it led to celebration. All of these possibilities--and many others--are there for us within the realm of art.

Notes

1. Emily Dickinson, "1129," *Anthology of American Literature:Volume II Realism to the Present,* ed. by George McMichael (New York: MacMillan Publishing Co., 1974), 194.

Essay 3

Art

> Yes, let the supreme norm for human art be, not conformity to tradition, not novelty or actuality, but *humanity:* a humanity grounded, protected and secretly secure in divinity; a humanity which has practical consequences for human fellowship, for relations with our fellow men and with nature.[1]

> Hans Kung

With the rapid introduction of new artistic styles, new media, new conceptual frameworks, old definitions of art no longer apply. As a result, authorities cannot agree about what constitutes art. Viewers are often confused when they find the unexpected object or event now labeled by the "authorities" as art.

I don't propose to come up with a new definition for art or to solve the many problems concerning the use of the term by contemporary theologians, philosophers or art historians. Instead, I will let those who think of themselves as artists and consider what they make to fit beneath the umbrella labeled "art" answer this question by example. But this approach is not universally sanctioned. Arthur Danto, for example, has proposed that art, from a philosophical perspective, is finished. He puts it this way:

> My thought was that art came to an end when it achieved a philosophical sense of its own identity, and that meant that an epic quest, beginning some time in the latter part of the nineteenth century, had achieved closure.[2]

Danto goes on to explain that art has not ended, but in reality art is no longer dominated by any particular artistic imperative. Or in other words, for artists, anything and everything is allowed.[3] George Dickie has provided a more pragmatic approach. As he sees it, anything that anyone who is a member of the art community nominates as art is art.[4] Dickie's approach certainly allows for a great deal of expansion and flexibility.

Populist or anti-elitist players wish to do away with all boundaries to art--they wish to consider almost anything that is made by humans to be art. For example, Roy Ascott asserts, "Art is now a form of behavior."[5] Walter De Maria, apparently with serious intent, claims that "meaningless work is obviously the most important and significant art form today."[6] This last approach to art consists not of refining a definition, but rather of de-defining a definition.   De-definition was borrowed by a number of art historians, such as Taylor for *America as Art*, or Martland for *Religion as Art*, who wish to blur boundaries rather than define them.

So how can we speak of Christian imagery, subjects and content in an intellectual environment that prefers to unfocus rather than focus our attention? If we borrow an idea from psychoanalysis, we can at least come to an understanding of the term "art" that will let us proceed.

A healthy individual maintains healthy boundaries.   Perhaps a healthy discipline such as art also needs to maintain its boundaries. Interpersonal and even inter-disciplinary relationships are essentially determined in relation to boundaries.   How we relate interpersonally is to a large extent shaped by our earliest relationships.   Good early interpersonal relationships with primary caregivers provide the child with a sense of self, or in other words create self-definition.   When the relationships are negative, the child

> . . . becomes vulnerable to *self-fragmentation* because his affect states have not been met with the requisite responsiveness from the caregiving surround.   And thus cannot become integrated into the organization of his self-experience.[7]

Thus psychoanalysis is about awareness of boundaries--about self-definition.   The healthy individual has appropriate boundaries for the situations that he or she may confront.   A person with weak boundaries becomes a tool of or slave to others.   A person with citadel-like boundaries can never know or be known by another.   Yet there are times when strong boundaries are necessary, as when the individual is confronted by an abusive personality.   And there are times when the appropriate boundary is flexible and more open, as when the individual is interacting with a good friend, a spouse, or her or his child.   In sum, the healthy individual respects the boundaries of others and maintains boundaries that are appropriate to the immediate situation.

It may follow then that those who wish to make a citadel-like fortress of art are overly protective of art.   Alternatively those who open all of the gates and allow anything in or out are overly permissive in their attitude towards what art may be or become.   Overly strong boundaries lead to rigidity and stagnation.   Weak or non-existent boundaries lead to severe abuse and ultimately to fragmentation.

Strong boundaries, with their obvious limitations, do at least provide definition. We know where the walls are and can differentiate between what is inside and outside the walls. With weak boundaries there is blurring. We can no longer be sure about what is or is not contained because the container itself has become virtually membrane free. With a totally permissive situation there are no boundaries, and whatever may have been contained is no longer contained. In fact, without boundaries art cannot exist. Dickie provides art with weak boundaries; then Taylor and Martland seek to eliminate them altogether.

Boundary issues are not unique to psychoanalysis or art. All disciplines are confronted with the tension of self-definition. And as long as language is one of our better tools for discussion, it seems that de-definition only destroys the possibility of communication. To intentionally de-define rather than re-define the terms we have no choice but to use is destructive--even self-destructive--an unhealthy approach to take for anyone but a confirmed nihilist.

Those who would de-define language also seem to be at odds with another aspect of Postmodernism. In Postmodern times we are admonished, with some legitimate justification, to become more socially aware and thus politically correct in our use of language. Could it be that those who wish to weaken language or radically de-define it are actually imperialist wolves in sheep's clothing?

Weak or undefined boundaries for art can lead to unfettered immigration and emigration, or it can become a prelude to an eventual hostile takeover. Either possibility seems inevitably to run counter to political correctness. For one choice leads to homogenization and the other is merely old-fashioned deceit. And either way inevitably destroys the more fragile and more vulnerable human traditions and cultural entities.

So I propose that we continue to allow art to have boundaries: and that we do not allow art to become imperialistically all encompassing. I propose that we continue to carefully scrutinize all new entities that are nominated as art, and not merely allow everything in.

We as artists, critics, curators and art historians need to remain vigilant, constantly examining the way we define what it is we speak of when we speak of art. Otherwise, we will cease to have anything to speak of. On the other hand, I do not suggest that we build a wall around the idea of art and make it a fossil. Then art could only be spoken of in the past tense.

If I did not suggest moderation in defining art, then I would not be allowed to take on the study of Christian Art using the present tense or the future tense.   For mainstream art history and criticism, though it may wear the guise of flexibility, has not been willing (through omission or commission) to open wide its gates to the discussion of contemporary Christian Art.

Notes

1. Hans Kung, *Art and the Question of Meaning,* trans. by Edward Quinn (New York: Crossroad, 1981), 50.

2. Arthur C. Danto, "Art after the End of Art," *Embodied Meanings: Critical Essays and Aesthetic Meditations* (New York: Farrar Straus Grioux, 1994), 324.

3. Danto, 328-330.

4. Danto, 312.

5. Roy Ascott, "Behaviourables and Futurables," *Theories and Documents of Contemporary Art: A Sourcebook of Artists' Writings,* ed. by Kristine Stiles and Peter Selz (Berkeley: University of California Press, 1996), 491.

6. Walter De Maria, "Meaningless Work," *Theories and Documents of Contemporary Art: A Sourcebook of Artists' Writings,* ed. by Kristine Stiles and Peter Selz (Berkeley: University of California Press, 1996), 526.

7. Robert D. Stolorow, Bernard Brandshaft and George E. Atwood, *Psychoanalytic Treatment: An Intersubjective Approach* (Hillsdale, New Jersey, The Analytic Press: 1987), 67.

Essay 4

Imagination

I've discovered that many Christians, perhaps especially evangelicals, fear imagination. Just last year, it occurred to me why. In the King James Version, which many Christians use as their only translation, imagination is always a bad word.[1]

Madeleine L'Engle

We are all images of God formed in God's imagination. Imagination, that ability to conceive mentally and then create, is the genesis of the universe. God's imagination is limitless and God can create a universe from nothing.

We human artists do not have God's infinite capacity for imagination, nor can we create something out of nothing. We can, however, use our imaginations to make artworks that direct attention to both God's infinite imaginative capacity and God's vast creative powers. We cannot speak and through our words bring into being anything so immense or complex as the universe and its diverse parts. But we can imagine artworks of great beauty, artworks that foster powerful emotions or artworks that express intellectual insights with subtlety and grace. Why then do we fear the imagination?

The answer is clear. Our human imagination can lead to what is good and beautiful and grace-filled. Our human imagination can also lead to what is ugly and deceitful and base. That is why Christians have often questioned the use of the imagination, especially as it relates to the arts.

Since the human imagination is capable of conceiving evil, it must be, according to some, restrained. It is fear that motivates this desire to restrain the imagination. And it is a fear that can cite evidence to support itself. But can the imagination turn to evil if the artist has placed the imagination of her heart and soul and mind within the hands of God? No!

Yet how can we be sure that a particular artist works within the grace of God? We can't. For as imperfect beings we are unable to dwell at all times in his grace. The cracks and crevices in our fallen humanness leave us vulnerable to evil. Even though we may be weak, does this mean that the seeds of the imagination planted in us by God should not be cultivated and nurtured and tended?

If the potential for evil were reason enough to restrain us from attempting what might be good or loving or fulfilling, then none of us would be able to do anything. The desire to draw people closer to God through preaching has turned some people away from God and also brought others closer to God. Does this mean that preaching should be forbidden?

Imaginative use of our God-given gifts contains the potential for good or evil. And no human act or venture or undertaking, including art, is totally filled with good, because our human imperfections may warp or blur our efforts. However, if the artist aims at truth telling, strives to give his best, and remains open to God, then much that is life-affirming may result.

How does the artist create life-affirming work? How does the artist stimulate her imagination? First the imagination must be freed of the many "I can'ts," the "I shouldn'ts," that we have been filled with. On the other hand, the imagination must also be freed from the "I shoulds," the "I musts," that also hold the imagination in check.

Freedom is a gift given each of us by Jesus, so that we might no longer be restrained by legalism. He also wants each of us to scrape away the unnecessary accretions that keep us from seeing, from hearing and from knowing truth. Our awareness is dulled by the thoughts and actions of others that would have us conform to their images of what we should be.

Instead, the freedom of Christ allows us to separate the false notions of self from the true notions of self. Freedom begins with the removal of false notions. Many who fear the imagination would prefer that the artist remain a captive of tradition or comfortable societal norms or some other cultural dogma. And while Christ does not advocate gratuitous destruction of traditions, societal norms or dogma, he does model dispensing with anything that would obscure or blunt or cover the truth about God and God's creation.

But isn't there a danger in allowing such freedom? Yes, but it would be even more dangerous to deny artists, or anyone else, the opportunity to seek after truth. Such seeking will cause discomfort. It will require that each of us think and love and forgive. And we may at times resent the inconvenience of it all, but any other option would cause even more pain and suffering.

How do we cultivate a flourishing artistic imagination? Freedom is a necessary piece. The freedom to imagine is not the end--it is rather the beginning. If our artistic imaginations are to grow they must be nurtured. Experience is a good teacher of the imagination. Go new places, do new things! Go to old places and look at them through the eyes of your new freedom. Do old things, but experience them in relation to your new freedom.

This is not a call to do everything and go every place. This is not a permission slip to do everything that comes to mind. Each person, each artist is given freedom, not for freedom's sake. The goal is to seek truth and then discern effective ways to image that truth or otherwise embody it. I am not going to propose a set of rules, nor am I going to draw up guidelines. Prayerful consideration with the Knower of all truth is far superior to anything I might propose, if truth-seeking is the goal.

If these experiences are to fill and nourish the imagination, the artist, as experiencer, must become aware. Awareness is not an all or nothing condition. No human is capable of being totally aware all of the time. However, if we are not aware, we will not be fed by our experiences.

There is no sure path that will lead all of us towards greater awareness. Yet some paths to awareness are worth trying. One very simple technique is to give yourself time and space to become focused on where you are and who you are. Take the time to see, to hear, to touch, to taste, to feel what is before you, whether it is a flower-filled garden in the springtime--or--the city dump in the midst of a hot and humid summer.

Take the time to be where you are and allow that place to make its presence known to you. Watch yourself as you respond to both isolated aspects of the place or combinations of these aspects. If you are drawn to memories or to thoughts of other places, acknowledge each of these and gently draw your attention back to the present now. Our imaginations will remain uninformed unless we make the room necessary; until we allow ourselves to experience our present time and place,.

Awareness of our surroundings is important. But awareness of how each of us responds to what surrounds us may be even more important.

How does each particular sensation or event or interaction touch us? Do we become melancholy or angry or joyful?

This kind of awareness is essential if the imagination is to serve us well.   An unaware individual has an uninformed imagination. Awareness gives us some insight into how others may respond to the art that we make.   It will not give us a full picture, but it can at least provide necessary knowledge.   The awareness of interactions between viewer and artwork will also work to keep each of us humble, as we realize that not all people will respond or even interact with our artworks--artworks into which we have poured the best we have to offer.

In addition to observing the ways viewers respond to what we make, it is good to observe how we respond to the art others have made.   It is valuable to interact with an artwork a number of times.   This will allow us to gauge the consistency of an artwork's impact.   Even keeping notes and comparing them may open us to the variability of our responses.   Some artworks may evoke a similar response no matter how often we view them, while other artworks may evoke varied responses that are highly dependent upon our own mood.   Some works may act more like a mirror than others.   This mirror-like quality is neither good nor bad.   It is, however, useful to be aware of how some artworks can appear to be more chameleon-like than others.

We should realize that our response to any particular artwork tells us as much about ourselves as it does about the artwork.   If we are put off by it, then we might study it to determine why we respond as we do.   I don't mean that we should try to change our response, though this may happen.   What I mean is that we should look inside ourselves to determine what it is that offends us in this artwork.

Some artworks are meant to bring offense; the artist means to challenge some part of our perceptual framework.   There are times when it is necessary to beat us over the head in order to draw our attention to something we would rather ignore than see.   If we look inside ourselves we may find that we hold within us irrational fears, intellectual misconceptions or spiritual blind spots to which we cling. This realization or new awareness may indeed be painful.   That does not mean we should shrink from the task.

Fortunately, we may also direct our awareness--sensual, intellectual and spiritual--to artworks when our initial response is pleasure. Becoming aware is not merely another grueling masochistic enterprise. It can draw us closer to what delights or inspires us too.   If our study of the artworks we enjoy is to have value for us, then it is good to attempt to discern why we respond the way we do. Of course there are times that we should make no attempt to analyze our individual responses. There are times when we should merely allow ourselves to be present with an artwork, to allow ourselves to respond to it as we would a dance partner.

Notes

1. Madeleine L'Engle, "Listening to the Story: A Conversation with Madeleine L'Engle," Interview by Dee Dee Risher, *The Other Side* 34(March & April 1998): 37.

Essay 5

Seeing

Seeing is not a substitute for speech; but it is a sensibility and modality in its own right, enriching in every way.   But it comes only out of repeated seeing, out of a practiced discipline as rigorous as learning to write or to become a writer.[1]

John Dillenberger

Our culture daily floods us with a multitude of visual images.   But even though most of us have grown up in the United States amidst these images, we are not skilled at seeing.   And by seeing I mean apprehending visually rather than seeing as understanding.   (We are so captivated by the instantaneous that we are not skilled at understanding either.)

Our lives are dominated by written and spoken words because they are so useful for communicating a wide range of ideas and emotions. Our schools emphasize reading and writing because this is currently the dominant mode of human communication.   Reading is important because we cannot remember important and significant information about history or law or religion.   There is too much information for any one mind to contain.   As a result we have become word dependent.

If we fail to gain adequate reading skills, our culture will push us to the side and label us as slow or lacking in motivation.   Unfortunately our quest for verbal literacy has resulted in other deficits.   Our educational system, so focused on books and computers, often stops including music or art education after the early primary years.   Since art is elective, not required, in our middle schools and high schools, it is no wonder that many of us are visually illiterate.   Consequently many of us are unable to see the value of art, for our culture makes it clear we do not need visual literacy.

When visual literacy is considered elective everyone suffers.   For visual artists it means the audience for their art is small.   It means that our culture shuts its eyes to a large body of human input.   It means that those who communicate with paint or stone or fabric or any other visual media are most often ignored or dismissed, not because what they have to say is irrelevant, but because so many of the audience have chosen either consciously or unconsciously to remain visually illiterate.

Some will argue that our culture is skilled at seeing as a result of cinema, television, video and digital imagery.   There is some truth in this since each of these media has a significant visual presence.   At the same time, however, most cinema, video and digital imagery is dominated by verbal communication.   Films are dominated by dialogue, by sequentially scripted narratives, or by graphic text. Seldom in mainstream productions is the visual allowed to dominate. Such experimentation is most often relegated to alternative venues.

Thus in our highly verbal culture we can watch cinema, video or digital media and still get by with a low level of visual literacy.   For we can depend upon the text to bail us out.   We can get the main point, we can follow the story, but we may miss many of the subtleties of visual communication.   We don't notice how a skilled director uses lighting to hide or reveal, or how a shift in viewpoint may affect our emotional response to a particular character.

And God, as the ultimate director, did not send us a story or video about Jesus, he sent Jesus.   Seeing Jesus, even touching him, was as important as hearing him!

How do we gain visual literacy?   We pursue it like we do anything else we want to learn.   First of all seeing requires spending time, slowing down.   We open ourselves to the visual world by sitting in one place long enough to really see how light and color and texture fill our eyes.   When we have learned to see with our eyes, we will be better prepared also to see with our hearts.

We must allow ourselves to spend as much time looking at and seeing a painting or sculpture as we spend on reading a book.   This may sound extreme, but it is not.   I am not asking you to stare at an artwork.   I am asking you to see it, to allow it into your mind through your eyes.   If we begin with the most or complex drawings or assemblages, we are likely to give up.   How many of us chose to read *The Brothers Karamazov* as our first venture into the novel?

The discipline of learning to see is easier if you begin with a visual object for which you feel some affinity--spiritual, emotional or intellectual.   If you choose something too foreign to your personality, you may reject it before you give yourself the chance to form a friendship. You may want to begin with visual poems or short stories rather than a visual novel--perhaps a simple ceramic vase, still life painting or drawing. Imagine yourself taking the place of the printmaker or weaver who formed the print or weaving before you. Imagine the personality of the artist. Seek to discern what motivated her to use this shade of green or why the left side of the piece is blurred and vague while the upper right is precise and focused. There is no one path that will work equally well for each viewer.

Yet if you aspire to visual literacy, you must do so actively. It has some similarities to reading. When you read a book, you do not just stare blankly at the page hoping that the meaning within the text will jump out and pull you in. Instead, you must actively proceed from one word to the next, one line to the next. If you are to make sense of these words, you must remember what you read so that you may make sense of what follows.

Reading is not a passive activity; neither is seeing. To see, you take into account the relationships between forms: values (lights and darks), textures, colors, lines, shapes. These relationships are no more accidental than the relationships of words within a text. If the artwork is representational, you must begin to notice what is depicted and how.

You may want to engage the artwork in dialogue. Introduce yourself. Ask the artwork questions. Seeing is interactive; it is not a monologue. You will begin to notice that some artists' works are more inviting (for you) than others. Some artworks are brusque while others are friendly and others are seductive. Artworks may or may not resemble the humans who made them; they can range from humble to arrogant.

But you may not notice these differences in visual personalities and how this affects communication until your seeing skills have been developed through practice. It is this practice that will lead to a fuller experiencing of artworks. Once our visual experience is widened, our visual vocabulary increases and we see more fully all that we see, whether it is on the face of a friend or at a scenic viewpoint.

Yet the reason for seeing is not merely for the sake of looking at art. We do not read merely so that we may read novels or histories. We read to gain information, to gain insight, to gain an understanding of our place in the world, to gain an understanding of our relationships to other living breathing human beings and to deepen our relationship with God.

We use sight to the same end.   By learning to see well, we enlarge our capacity to gain the visual information so central to understanding. With deepened understanding we can appreciate and enrich our relationships with both nature and society.   More significantly, we can learn to see God through creation.   And we can better see and understand those who wear the face of Jesus behind the individualized and contradictory masks their human personalities have crafted.

There is no advocacy here of "art for art's sake."   Art is not the end, it is a means--a means capable of richness and depth and power.

Notes

1. John   Dillenberger, "Religion and the Sensibilities of the Artist,"   *Faith and Form* (Autumn 1978): 24.

Essay 6

Iconoclasm

Art is bitterly iconoclastic; it opposes the phony, the empty, and the outrageous in life: thus does it ruthlessly demolish the dead wood of convention--and thus does it search for new images of the strange reality of nature, ourselves, and the sacred amid which we live.[1]

Langdon Gilkey

We seldom think of the artist as an iconoclast in the context of the history of Christianity.   Clearly language is a plastic and flexible medium, for the traditional meaning of iconoclast is an individual who finds visual imagery within the Church to be anathema.   But Gilkey has brought our attention to a significant issue.   Because he uses iconoclasm in a different way, he forces us to think about what it involves.

Both types of iconoclast, either the image-maker or the image-destroyer, have something in common.   Each is concerned with truth. The Christian iconoclast is concerned that believers will worship the image rather than the truth it represents, while the artistic iconoclast is concerned that art be freed from principles or stylistic conventions that would limit the artist's ability to image truth.

Both the artistic and Christian iconoclast desire to place life over death.   For an image is not alive, it cannot begin to compare with a living being or a living and holy spirit.   In a similar way stylistic conventions and principles, when they are adhered to blindly, will very likely ensure dead art.

Artists working with Christian subjects, content or imagery often face both types of iconoclasm.   On the one hand, the fruit of an artist's life and work may be rejected because visual imagery of any kind is deemed suspect by church bodies or entire denominations. There are a variety of theological rationales for keeping worship image free. Patrick Henry, in the guise of a question, points to one major objection Christians have used to justify iconoclasm in the church:

> Is the material world--the world accessible through the senses of sight, touch, smell, hearing, tasting--an illusion, to be obliterated by the truth revealed in Christ? There have been many Christians who have, to one degree or another, thought so, and for them art is necessarily a distraction, a pulling down of the soul which should be leaping up above the world of sense to the God who is pure spirit.[2]

Many modern Christians unknowingly adhere to the Gnostic heresy, to which Henry refers above, which emphasizes the supremacy of pure spirit over physical reality. And because the visual arts are so tangible and physical, they become particularly suspect. On the other hand written or spoken words, though less tangible and concrete, are ostensibly a safer means of devotion, worship and general communication. Yet the Gnostic iconoclast is not the only variety found in a Christian setting.

The Biblical commandment against the use of graven images is also used to deny the arts entry into the church. The second commandment reads, "Thou shalt not make unto thee any graven image, or any likeness of *anything* that *is* in heaven above, or that *is* in the earth beneath, or that *is* in the water under the earth"(Ex 20:4, AV). In the King James (Authorized) Version the injunction against image making is clear.

Yet in other translations the injunction against image making is obviously limited to idols: "You shall not make for yourself an idol, whether in the form of anything that is in heaven above, or that is on the earth beneath, or that is in the water under the earth"(Ex 20:4). The second translation seems to mesh with God's commands for his people to craft and ornament the Ark of the Covenant, the temple in Jerusalem and the Brazen Serpent. This second Biblical commandment has (even by conservative Christian writers) been interpreted not to refer to graven images *per se,* but as against the worship of anything other than God.[3] God's image was, even then, rampant on earth since each individual human is made in God's image.

How one interprets this commandment must also take into account the New Testament with the new covenant. And Jesus, who is at the center of this covenant, is physically concrete (incarnate) and is also the created image of God.   If God's image is completely forbidden on earth, then how can Christ's existence--or that of any other human form made in God's image--on earth be explained?   An over strict interpretation of the second commandment seems unconvincing when viewed in context.

Even if an artist can come to terms with church-based iconoclasm, she or he must still discern how to become an iconoclast that would confront the cozeners, those merchants of death so prevalent in any historical period.   How does the artist discern what to draw from the well of tradition?   How does the artist make it clear that the well is empty or poisoned?

Has the answer been pointed to by Picasso?   He said: "In my case a picture is a sum of destructions.   I do a picture--then I destroy it."[4] Actually,

> Picasso said that every work of creation begins with an act of destruction.   The artist is as much iconoclast as icon builder; the work of the artist involves the destruction of old models of reality in order to prepare the way for new ones.   The artist is one who excludes no possibility in human experience and yet (in humility) recognizes nothing as absolute or sacrosanct.   The artist is not an idolator.
>
> The artist is not an idolator.   "To have no graven images " means that no concepts, doctrines, mental sets, or cultural patterns are allowed to block the free flow of the visionary process.   The attempt to make a plastic or verbal work of art is not against the spirit of the commandment so long as the thing made remains a message/icon pointing beyond itself, transparent to the power of Life itself in creation.[5]

It might be more accurate to say that the artists are not idolators when they are true to their calling.   Merely being an artist does not preclude idolatry.

If we objectively consider twentieth century art, we might conclude that an iconoclastic stance was indeed the preferred if not required stance.   In many instances this led to vitality.   For the stranglehold of invalid traditions was put aside.   However, in other instances everything was destroyed.   Everything from previous centuries was reviled.

This was certainly the case for the Futurists, even if we take into account the constant hyperbole used by Marinetti, the Futurists' chief apologist.   He advocated a clean sweep.   "We will glorify war--the only true hygiene of the world--militarism, patriotism, the destructive gesture of the anarchist."[6] My point is that we humans can idolize iconoclasm.   Thus whatever stance we take, we need to constantly reexamine our motivations, so that we unveil truth rather than the face of death hiding behind a simulacrum of truth.

If an artwork leads us to celebrate and worship God more fully, or if an artwork gives us a better understanding of God or a better understanding of how God would have us live, then it has served a vital and useful function.   In addition, if an artwork leads us to see more fully the beauty of God's creation, or to see more fully the image of God in each human face, or to become more aware of the presence of the Holy Spirit among us, then our faith is enhanced and sustained.

On the other hand, if an artwork exposes deceit, or makes us aware of the evil that is present in our midst, or calls us to change our lives in a way that would be pleasing to God, then it has served a truly spiritual purpose.   Art, like many other human activities, has the potential to enliven communal life for Christians.   Artists need to open themselves to the input of community members.   They need also to think diligently, develop skills continually, and remain open to the touch of God's spirit.   It is not an easy task, but then neither is life itself.

Iconoclasm that inveighs against images is, in the end, a defensive posture.   It is more concerned with keeping something evil out than with letting what is good enter.   This type of iconoclasm, over time, can lead to idolatry--idolizing the defensive posture.   Iconoclasm that seeks to unveil the truth behind our lives is in the end, an offensive posture more concerned with uprooting evil than with constructing something that is wholesome and good.   This kind of iconoclasm, over time, can lead to an idolatry of the offensive posture itself.   As in many areas of life balance may be the answer, but not balance for its own sake, rather a balance that allows us the time and the space to see reality.

Perhaps the iconodules, those men and women who valued images, have the answer.

If the material creation is good, and if God really came into it, it follows that iconodules are less in error than iconoclasts.   The human capacity for idolizing the works of our hands, which is feared by the iconoclasts, is less virulent than the human capacity for pride in "spiritual" superiority.   Biblical religion may be threatened by apparent breaches of the Second Commandment, but biblical religion is undone by denials of the goodness of creation, and of the hearing-tasting-touching-smelling-seeing reality of the incarnation.[7]

Iconodules have taken a positive stance in relation to images and creation itself. Instead of locking out whatever has the potential to corrupt, they welcome whatever has the potential to enhance Christian worship and celebration. Instead of attacking what is corrupt, they embrace and celebrate the wholeness of God's creation.

But a complete community needs all three stances. The iconoclastic purifier takes on the role of defender of the faith. The iconoclastic scourge takes on the role of prophetic opponent of evil. The reconciling iconodule takes on the role of healing and Godly revelry. In our time cynicism and skepticism dominate the arts. We need to encourage and support those who take on the role of iconodule. For those women and men would fill our places of worship with artworks that heal our world, and link our hearts and minds with the heart and mind of God.

Notes

1. Langdon Gilkey, "Can Art Fill the Vacuum," *Art, Creativity, and the Sacred: An Anthology in Religion and Art*, ed. by Diane Apostolos-Cappadona (New York: Crossroad, 1984), 191.

2. Patrick Henry, "Religion and Art: The Uneasy Alliance," *Religion in Life* (Winter 1980): 452.

3. Francis A. Schaeffer, *Art and the Bible: Two Essays* (Downers Grove, Illinois: InterVarsity Press, 1973), 11.

4. Pablo Picasso, "Conversations," *Theories of Modern Art: A Sourcebook by Artists and Critics*, ed. by Herschel B. Chipp (Berkeley: University of California Press, 1968), 267.

5. Jay C. Rochelle, "Proclamation and Vision: Notes toward Ministry to Artists," *Dialog* (Spring 1981): 93.

6. F. T. Marinetti, "The Foundation and Manifesto of Futurism," *Theories of Modern Art: A Sourcebook by Artists and Critics*, ed. by Herschel B. Chipp (Berkeley: University of California Press, 1968), 286.

7. Henry, p. 458.

Essay 7

Artists

> The artist is placed on the stage of existence by God, there to do his or her work of making and selecting so as to bring forth something of benefit and delight to other human beings, something in acknowledgment of God.[1]

Nicholas Woltersdorf

What makes an artist Christian? Is there Christian art? Neither of these questions is easily answered, because any answer should be built upon a foundation of clear presuppositions. I ask both questions at the same time--for the answer to the first affects significantly the answer to the second—and examine several proposed answers before coming to tentative conclusions.

"What makes an artist Christian?" is ultimately not for humans to answer in the sense of judging the Christian-ness of a particular artist. For God is the only judge capable of seeing the whole soul and being of any individual person, artist, doctor or plumber. Yet, I think that the question can be resolved. The simplest answer is that if an artist self-labels herself as a Christian, then she is a Christian artist. While this solution is a good beginning, it lacks depth and substance; it is too much like what we might choose for a multiple-choice question in the "objective" section of an exam. Such a one-sentence answer, though rational, is not satisfying. It needs to be given flesh.

The popular press, including the popular Christian press, relies heavily on the artist's use of art as a vehicle for witnessing, in determining the appropriateness of the label Christian. In a brief article in *Christian Life,* a Native-American artist is extolled because "for the last few years this Tsimsian Indian has been using his artistic talents to witness for Christ."[2]

In another instance, Max Greiner, best known for his sculpture *Divine Servant,* is commended as a Christian artist.   According to Ken Walker, writing for *Charisma,*

> *Divine Servant* is more than a sculpture.   Max Greiner is an example of how one man who yielded to God's direction discovered an unusual avenue for ministry to thousands of people.   It also proves that lay people can reach others for Christ through their careers.[3]

In both these instances the writers imply that if the artist produces art that draws people to Christ, then the maker is a Christian artist. However, it would be unfair to ascribe too much value to these implied definitions, since the writers of both articles were not necessarily attempting determine, "What makes an artist Christian?"

Calvin Seerveld, in the Reformed tradition, answers this question by elaborating on the role of art within a Christian context.   For him if the artist is fulfilling this role then he or she is a Christian artist.   For Seerveld, art can serve either of two functions:

> Since the very creation of the world the problem has been whether these arts have been fashioned and used by men and women as vehicles of praise to the Lord, or whether they have been conceived and executed as expressions of human vanity.[4]

Seerveld wants fruits to determine the label an artist will eventually be given.

Seerveld's concept of fruits is more profound than that found in the popular press.   He expands it beyond the role of drawing people to Christ.   For Seerveld,

> Christian art chartered by the Bible may bring to canvas and book and modulated tones anything afoot in the world, in a way that shall expose sin . . . waste [condemned by God] and show obedient life as a joy forever, thereby building up the faithful and making strangers to the faith curious and desirous of joining in such reconciling fun in our Father's world.[5]

If an artist works with this intention and her art results in a *"fused presentation of knowledge necessarily rich in suggestion,"*[6] or in other words the artwork is artistic in its making, then she is indeed a Christian artist.

Madeleine L'Engle adds flesh to the skeleton of the objective answer when she writes, "I am beginning to see that almost every definition I find of being a Christian is also a definition of being an artist."[7] If an artist strives to approach his life and his art as one integrated whole, as a seamless fabric in which the goals of life and art-making are totally interwoven, then he is a Christian artist. We cannot, L'Engle implies, separate out the parts of the individual humanness of the artist without distorting or destroying our experience of that humanness. It is in the making itself that the artist can discover what God and humanness are, or in L'Engle's own words:

> To serve a work of art is almost identical with adoring the Master of the Universe in contemplative prayer. In contemplative prayer the saint (who knows himself sinner, for none of us is whole, healed and holy twenty-four hours a day) turns inwards in what is called "the prayer of the heart: not to find self but to lose self in order to be found."[2]

I believe that L'Engle would not limit such work to artists alone, it is applicable to any work of vocation. It is when the artist becomes the servant of the work that artistic creation is really possible. It is then that "the work is better than the artist."[9] For the artist finds a way of transcending self by abandoning the trappings of self so that true self is revealed. L'Engle strongly implies that if the artist focuses on self-- including taking on the label of Christian artist--then the resulting art will speak only of self rather than transcend self.

Jacques Maritain also warns of focusing on the self-label as Christian when he writes:

> If you want to produce Christian work, be a Christian, and try to make a work of beauty into which you have put your heart; do not adopt a Christian pose. Do not make the absurd attempt to sever in yourself the artist and the Christian. They are one, if you really are a Christian, and if your art is not isolated from your soul by some aesthetic system. But apply only the artist in you to the work in hand; precisely because they are one, the work will be as wholly of the one as of the other.[10]

Both Maritain and L'Engle provide a holistic description of how the artist is a Christian artist. It is only in the actual making of art that the artist gives proof to his or her Christianity. And it is a proof that does not wear a badge.   It may in fact be a proof that the artist has not fully understood, if the artist has not died to self in the process of art making.

We have looked at three ways of answering our first question, "What makes an artist Christian?"   The answer can be the artist's Christian witness or ministry, it can be the artist's fulfillment of a Biblical mandate to bear fruit, and it can be reflected in the artist's holistic merging of beliefs and vocation.   In truth none of these definitions excludes the others, each merely places more or less emphasis on defining aspects.

Writers supporting the second and third approaches provide a more complex and complete image of the Christian artist.   Their definitions focus on the context of vocation, and a whole life journey, rather than on an activity with a stated goal or purpose.

Seerveld is more emphatic about fruits or goals than either L'Engle or Maritain.   But he is broad enough to allow for a wide range of artistic results.   On the other hand, L'Engle and Maritain put more emphasis on getting the self out of the way.   They stress making art within the embrace of faith, but without a preconceived itinerary or agenda.   And, to a great extent, Seerveld is concerned with establishing what that embrace of faith is, within the mind of the artist.

It seems to me that if the artist combines what Seerveld, L'Engle and Maritain present into a single definition, then the result will also encompass that represented in the popular press.   Artists who are informed of their God-given role, who are able to reach beyond the self from the vantage point of faith, will indeed create art that witnesses fully to God's love of humankind and all creation.

Now we move to the question, "Is there Christian art?"   We have discussed what might make an artist Christian.   But does it necessarily follow that art made by Christian artists is Christian?   Ronald B. Allen comes to the conclusion that "In the last analysis art is not 'Christian.' Things are not Christian, people are."[11] I could stop right here, because Allen has made an excellent point, but first we need to consider other possible answers.

Some influential writers, such as Francis Schaeffer, speak about the existence of Christian art and what that art should be about in the twentieth century, when he writes: "First, Christian art today should be twentieth-century art."[12] However Schaeffer more often speaks of "A Christian's art."[13] So when he writes about "Christian art," he may actually be referring to the Christianity of the artist, or of the presentation in art of a Christian world-view.

Another possibility is suggested by Sharlyn Welker Stare. She writes about the College Hill Presbyterian Church making an effort to "reclaim the arts" indicating that Christian art may, in a proprietary sense, be for and belong to Christians.[14]

More recently Steve Scott assumed the fact of Christian art when he wrote: "Characteristics of Christian art are empathetic and compassionate identification with fellow believers, and identification with the world of the non-believing viewer and hearer."[15] Later Scott warns:

> Christian artists need to ground their understanding of why they do what they do--their epistemology--in a clear and sober analysis of what Scripture teaches. If not, they will remain immature, "blown about by every wind of doctrine," and Christian art will be compromised by pragmatic agendas that have been dressed up in fine sounding "spiritual" language.[16]

Does Scott uses the term of Christian art merely to differentiate it from other artistic genres, as is the case for contemporary music where Jazz, Rock, Classical, Christian and Country Western genres are used mainly to help buyers avoid types of music they find unappealing? Or, as this quote implies, does he label art as Christian art if it has its basis in Scripture? The later seems more likely.

However, if we go back to Scott's earlier statement, then Christian art must also appeal to or at least allow identification with the non-believer as well as the Christian believer. Because Scott himself does not clarify what he means, we cannot be sure how he intends us to understand the designation "Christian art." So is the designation to be avoided because of the confusion such use engenders? Or are we left with the more awkward designation "art made by Christians"?

Art made by Christians does not declare in any way that objects/artworks are Christian. It is both troublesome and awkward as a designation. For is there anything *per se* different about art made by Christians that separates it from art made by non-Christians? We could hope that art made by Christians might, as Schaeffer indicates, somehow reflect a Christian worldview or perspective.

However, L'Engle does not agree: "*Christian* art? Art is art; a painting is a painting; music is music; a story is a story. If it is bad art, it's bad art, no matter how pious the subject."[17] Perhaps we are to conclude that if something--a story, a cantata or an etching—is well made, then the making of it was a positive and life-affirming action. And ultimately it reflects the truth of the creator.

Perhaps Christians who make art should not be overly concerned about the labels applied to the art they make.   Instead, each Christian artist should ground herself in Christian belief, open herself to God's input, and seek to understand humanity and its relationship with creation.   The art that then springs from her, if accomplished with thought and skill and humility, cannot help but reflect something of God.

Notes

1. Nicholas Woltersdorf, *Art in Action* (Grand Rapids, Michigan: William B. Eerdmans Publishing Company, 1980), 91.

2. Linda Hall, "Tsimsian Witness," *Christian Life* (July 1978): 45.

3. Ken Walker, "The Sculpture That Speaks," *Charisma* (October 1994): 55.

4. Calvin G. Seerveld, "Relating Christianity to the Arts," *Christianity Today* (November 7, 1980):48.

5. Calvin G. Seerveld, *Rainbows for a Fallen World* (Toronto: Tuppence Press, 1980), 33.

6. Calvin G. Seerveld, "Relating Christianity to the Arts," 49. Italics his.

7. Madeleine L'Engle, "Reflections on Faith and Art," *The Other Side* (December 1982): 12.

8. L'Engle, 12.

9. L'Engle, 12.

10. Jacques Maritain, *Art and Scholasticism,* trans. by J. F. Scanlan (New York: Scribner, 1954), 54.

11. Ronald B. Allen, " The Road to Distinction," *Discipleship Journal* 39 (1987): 33.

12. Francis A. Schaeffer, *Art & the Bible: Two Essays* (Downers Grove: InterVarsity Press, 1973), 50.

13. Schaeffer, 50.

14. Sharlyn Welker Stare, "Reclaiming the Reflections of the Creator," *Key to Christian Education* (Winter 1986): 1.

15. Steve Scott, *Like A House On Fire: Renewal of the Arts in a Postmodern Culture* (Chicago: Cornerstone Press Chicago, 1997), 54.

16. Scott, 61.

17. L'Engle, 10.

Essay 8

Beauty

> As with the experience of beauty in nature, unless the Christian faith
> has an understanding and place for the arts it will inevitably fail to win
> the allegiance of those for whom they are the most important aspect of
> life. For they will see in the Christian faith only what strikes them as
> flat, moralistic and platitudinous compared to the troubling, haunting
> depths of Mahler or *King Lear*. Unless the experience of beauty in
> nature and the arts is encompassed and affirmed the Christian faith will
> seem to have nothing of interest or importance to say. This is not
> however, just a tactic to win the allegiance of the lost. The fact is that
> God is beautiful and the Church is hiding this.[1]

> Richard Harries

Beauty as a concept has given twentieth century writers, especially
art critics and art historians, a great deal of difficulty. Why is this so?
Answering would take several volumes--I will settle for less.

The traditional idea of beauty has all the trappings of a universal
concept. For Plato, one of the earliest and most prominent supporters
of such universals, beauty, along with other concepts, had the mind of
the creator as its source. For much of Christianity's existence Plato's
idea of beauty was accepted--with some alterations. For one, the
creator became Yahweh, creator of the universe. Secondly, though
spiritual beauty might inhabit physical beauty, the reverse was not
necessarily the case.

The link between physical and spiritual beauty did however become
central for many artists and writers of the Renaissance. The
connection was weakened in the Baroque period, when beauty was
made to compete with emotional intensity and physical veracity. The
Enlightenment, which overlaps the art historical period of the Baroque,
brought beauty down to earth.

Some Enlightenment philosophers questioned the intellectual acceptability of belief in God. And without God, where could beauty exist? Certainly it must be in the eye of the beholder. Well, as long as each beholder has a different set of eyes, a different response to what is perceived, then beauty can no longer be adjudged universal. So as empiricist thought dominated the philosophical environment, the concept of beauty became less interesting and beauty in the arts became less crucial.

The Romantics, who were not impressed with empiricism, loved beauty, but it had to share their affections with the sublime (which was more thrilling) and the exotic (which was more seductive). The Materialists, including the Marxists, had no use for beauty. For it was a harlot who had sold out to the powerful and elitist forces that kept the rest of humankind in thrall.

Beauty as a concept has been so crippled by negative associations that it is now seen as synonymous with pretty or handsome. Such a weak term was of little use to those who vied for intellectual ascendancy in the twentieth century. Writing about the arts of the twentieth century focused on integrity, or conceptual innovation, uniqueness of vision or personal expression, social awareness, aesthetic diversity or psychological honesty--but not beauty. This does not mean that some of what beauty encompassed is not included. Rather it means that the term *beauty* is seen as anachronistic and no longer viable or meaningful within the current language of discussion.

But is this the case? The broadened scope allowed in a Postmodernist culture does not mandate abandoning beauty. If artists may make reference to art from the past, including that of ancient Greece and the Renaissance, then beauty may again be discussed. It will not likely be made the central focus, but it may play a supporting role.

One positive outcome is that beauty will again need to be redefined as it re-enters the intellectual marketplace. And as beauty is redefined, there is the chance that the concept of universals, and beauty as one of them, may become intellectually acceptable again. As a concept it may again been seen as viable.

Richard Harries, in *Art and the Beauty of God*, has made valuable connections between beauty, God and the arts for Christians. He re-universalizes the term *beauty* by identifying God as the ultimate beauty:

All that is, is fundamentally good; so all that is, radiates with the divine splendour. This means that truly to discern the existence of anything, whether a flower or a grain of sand, is to see its finite existence rooted in the ground of being, God himself; it is to discern glimmerings of eternal light, flames or flashes of divine beauty.[2]

Many of Harries' terms are absent from contemporary art history and criticism. *Good, splendor, eternal* and *divine* are not frequent visitors to most contemporary discussions of art because they indicate a divergent intellectual perspective. They are absent because their use assumes a God. And with a God, *beauty, good, eternal* and *divine* communicate ideas that transcend the individual personality.

Many if not most art historians and art critics adhere to alternative perspectives. So writers who use these terms to refer to universal concepts will have to use them with intelligence and precision. For any imprecision or lack of clarity will certainly and legitimately be exposed.

But if dealt with clearly, beauty may again be viewed as a legitimate concept in relation to contemporary art with Christian imagery, subjects or content. That would create new concerns to deal with. The first of these is that seekers after beauty will not go the distance, as Jenson suggests, and they will end up adoring beauty for its own sake. Then beauty will be disconnected from God its source:

> But Western history has gone on to teach another lesson as well: the experience of beauty does not survive the cessation of worship. Precisely those who thematically dedicate themselves to beauty, and who within the modern Western tradition regularly just so abandon worship, are in wave after wave driven at last to deny beauty as well.[3]

Beauty is anchored in God. Without belief in him, beauty is merely an empty shell filled with the hollow echoes of unrequited spiritual desires.

While seeking beauty for its own sake can lead us into a spiritual cul-de-sac, that is not the only danger. Another is that those seeking God will be seduced by beauty before they are sufficiently grounded in faith. This difficulty may arise if Christian believers are not made aware of the theological relationship between beauty and God. If they are not aware of God as the source of beauty, then Saliers believes that they may become confused: "we are on the brink of substituting the 'holiness of beauty' for religious concern with the beauty of holiness. Admiration for the artistic may prevent real prayer and worship."[4] Thus the worship of beauty diverts the believer from worshipping God, the source of both holiness and beauty.

So the worship of beauty can become the non-believer's substitute for the worship of God.   Or beauty can misdirect the worship of a believer.   Being made aware of beauty is somewhat akin to becoming familiar with fire.   Like fire, beauty is powerful, it can create inner warmth, it can surround us with brightness and light, it can allow us to see and follow a path through the dreary darkness that surrounds us. Or it can consume us if we abandon ourselves to it.

On the other hand, the absence of beauty, like the absence of fire, can leave us cold and hungry and unsatisfied.

> Admiration for the beauty without grasping the intrinsic and intimate connection with faith may lead to idolatry.   Such an attitude often correlates with the sentimental, the cheap and ersatz or with the pompous; hence we often have both aesthetic and religious faithlessness, [5]

warns Saliers.   On the other hand, recognizing that beauty exists only in God can lead to an eye-opening, soul-reviving revelation that brings joy to the heart and mind of the believer.

Notes

1. Richard Harries, *Art and the Beauty of God: A Christian Understanding* (London: Mowbray, 1993), 5-6.

2. Harries, 36.

3. Robert W. Jenson, "Beauty," *Dialog* (Fall 1986): 251.

4. Don E. Saliers, "Beauty and Holiness Revisited: Some Relations Between Aesthetics and Theology," *Worship* (May 1974): 288.

5. Saliers, 288.

Essay 9

Images

When we see Jesus, we become like him. So when the relationship
with Christ is once again established, there begins a life-long process.
This vocation of being transformed or transfigured into the likeness of
God is also a quality which the icon is communicating to us.[1]

Solrunn Nes

Seeing Jesus, to aspire to resemble him, is not a Protestant concept.
Protestants are more comfortable with words; we feel more at home
listening to Jesus' words. The WORD is the basis of our
understanding of whom Jesus is. Jesus is the WORD, and it is through
words that we come to know him. After all we have the record of
some of his spoken words, but we have no historically valid image. In
many instances our Protestant heritage is founded upon the destruction
of images, on ridding the churches of alleged idolatrous paintings and
sculptures, and upon whitewashed walls.

Whitewashed walls were seen as purification. With the walls blank
and white we could concentrate on the WORD and the words of the
preacher. We learned to hear, for the words of the new clergy were
now our own. And if the goal was to understand, then it was good to
be spoken to in a tongue we could understand. So our tongues danced
as our words became rich with comfort and admonition and prophecy.
And we allowed ourselves to speak through liturgy and prayer. We
allowed ourselves to sing words of praise.

But sometimes we got lost within this world of words. Sometimes
we wished for a more varied diet; we wanted to be fed by more than
sounds--we wanted to see. But we had closed our eyes so often in
prayer that when the preacher perseverated, our minds slept even if our
eyes remained open. We had put blinders on so that we could follow
the straight and narrow path to salvation without distraction. We had

plucked out our eyes rather than allow them to engage in sin, or we had become either myopic or farsighted. We could not see further than our next step, or we could see only our final goal.

Our eyes weakened by disuse failed us, for we lost the ability to see to discern the image of God in those who were different from us, in those who had been formed within another family or community. So most Protestants struggle to see; they have lost the ability to visualize, to image God's presence among them.

Now clearly this scenario is only partly true.

Imagine how different things might be if our families and communities venerated images of Jesus, of saints and of angels. But isn't that idolatry? Not according to Solrunn Nes, who says that icons are symbols: "The symbol should be venerated, and the reality, which is Christ himself, should be worshiped."[2] Some individual Orthodox worshipers may get confused, but the Orthodox Church has always been clear on the difference.

However, for those of us who are not Orthodox Christians, we may not know how to differentiate between veneration and worship. Our dictionary definitions of these words are not much help. If we equate veneration with reverence and worship with adoration, we may gain some sense of how to differentiate between veneration and worship. We can revere something, an icon for example, and admire it greatly without worshipping it.

On the other hand, worship goes beyond reverence. Worship is deeper and wider and all encompassing. When we worship something, we give ourselves fully and without restraint. When we venerate something, we may admire and respect it deeply, but we do not give ourselves over to this something unconditionally.

But don't icons encourage this confusion and lead the unwitting or confused into sin? Yes, this danger always exists, but there can be idolatry of the spoken or written word as well as the image. As humans we have evidenced the capacity to make idols of anything our minds can conceive. Idolatry is part of our fallen humanness.

Our senses can lead us either toward God or away from God. Each of us in each moment makes the choice between worshipping God or worshipping the idols of our choosing. Recognizing our propensity for idolatry may lead us to close ourselves off, to wall ourselves in for protection. Yet this wall may keep out what is life giving as well as what is life threatening.

We can instead choose to live in the world, surrounded by potential threats, as Jesus did. He chose not to send away the woman who washed his feet with her tears, even though her act was fraught with sensuality. While Simon the Pharisee remained within the wall of the law, Jesus chose to live in the moment, open to the good gifts that that freedom manifested. Simon saw only a harlot; Jesus saw a woman seeking forgiveness.

Yes, but how do icons and images fit with this story? It is easy to understand how narratives, like this one about Jesus and the woman who washed his feet, can act as a model for our behavior, but what has a visual image to offer? Narratives cannot show us the compassionate look of Christ or the disdain of Simon. A story cannot demonstrate the body language of acceptance or love. Now this does not mean that we should dispense with story with its sequential unfolding of history or parable. We do not need to cut out our tongue or plug up our ears so that we can only see.

However, God chose to illustrate and embody himself in the human form of Jesus, to make himself visible. He gave image to his WORD-- why shouldn't we follow his example? Why should we feel reluctant to make images of God's embodied self, of Jesus? If an image can help us visualize Jesus, then it can help us live out this image in our lives. In other words, images of Jesus can model for us what is Christ-like so that we might better see this image in others and wear this image ourselves. As Solrunn Nes suggests, icons can help us to transform ourselves, for as we focus on Jesus, we may come to see more fully what we are becoming in him.

Notes

1. "In the Image of God: An Interview with Solrunn Nes," *Areopagus* (Pentecost 1991): 35.
2. Ibid., 35.

Essay 10

Demons

Picasso, in breaking through the barriers of reality, opened a kind of Pandora's box. The spirits took their abode in the minds of men like Duchamp, and brought a whirlwind of anarchy, nihilism and the gospel of absurdity. The wind is still blowing, and is becoming a storm: a storm called revolution.[1]

H. R. Rookmaaker

How does the Christian who is an artist live in a culture and accept that which is good and reject that which is evil? Christian scholars and writers seldom agree on what is acceptable and what is objectionable. Paintings, assemblages, performance pieces, prints, sculptures and other artworks have spawned a vast and varied written response.

In 1978, H. R. Rookmaaker's response was one of careful, but severe questioning. Rookmaaker saw modernity in art as symptomatic of anti-rationality, nihilism and anarchy. Modern culture, in his view, is sick and must be rejected. On the other hand, Diane Apostolos-Cappadona finds that Modern art can provide a positive spiritual experience.[2]

Rookmaaker takes the opposite view when he writes of Jackson Pollock, perhaps the best known of the Abstract Expressionists. Rookmaaker writes "large canvases were painted 'abstractly' by dripping paint on them from a can as they lay on the ground, the end of a development in search of contentless art."[3]

Yet Apostolos-Cappadona asserts that these same Abstract Expressionists

break down the recognizable, the comfortable, the conventionally meaningful in order to create a reaction in us; to cause us to feel or see or think in new ways and new categories; and to experience ourselves and the world differently.[4]

Rookmaaker and Apostolos-Cappadona were not involved in a dialogue with each other, but they could have been. And most likely each would have dismissed the other's viewpoint, because each writer has taken a stance that allows little room for change--total rejection or total acceptance.

How does each of us deal with our desires to accept or reject what the art world and our culture offers or demands of us? We could write off those who hold a position opposite our own. I could label Rookmaaker a fundamentalist of the right and I could, on the other hand, label Apostolos-Cappadona a fundamentalist of the left. Rookmaaker seems, as is sometimes the case with conservatives, to fear the new. Appostolos-Cappadona seems, as is sometimes the case with liberals, to eagerly and readily accept the new. Yet this broad and sweeping approach to labeling opposing viewpoints does not seem to fit with a Christian model.

We are called at least to work toward seeing those who hold different views as individual humans. When we label before we look or listen, we cease to see or hear beyond the label we have applied. Would Rookmaaker claim that all Modern art is corrupt? The simple answer is no. In Rouault, a contemporary of Duchamp, he finds an artist who uses some aspects of modernity to communicate Christian compassion.[5] When we look and listen more closely, we find exceptions, we find some small points of agreement with those who express an opposite view. When we are open to seeing and listening, we can leave behind the walls that contain us and limit us--we can find freedom.

Does this mean that we should surround ourselves--our individualities--with a totally permeable membrane, that we must be open to everything? No! For doesn't freedom demand responsibility?

If we are to be responsible then we need to work towards understanding another person who holds a view different from our own. We are called to see and hear, but not to accept without first examining--without searching to separate what is true from what is untrue. If, after examining what another paints or sculpts or writes, we find some artwork or idea deficient in truth, should we then cut off this relational interaction? No! To continue dialogue with someone you disagree with is an act of love.

Jesus has called us to "love one another" (Jn 13:34), even to "love [our] enemies" (Lk 6:27). Seeing and listening, as well as speaking forthrightly, are ways that love can be expressed. So long as both parties continue to interact fully, both open to being influenced by the other and to influencing the other--in other words, true dialogue--then only good can come of it.   When one of the participants stops being open or gives up on influencing the other, dialogue ceases--perhaps until some future time.   If true dialogue is to continue, it must be recognized that a combative stance will undermine true dialogue.   All of this applies to three-way or group discussions as well.

But what has this to do with unmasking demons?   It points out that, even though demons do exist, often the demons we see are illusions. To call something demonic can be merely the placing of a label on something that we do not want to understand, out of disgust, fear or some other weakness.

Sometimes the worst demon we must confront is the one we view in the mirror.   To paraphrase Walt Kelly's Pogo, we have met the demons, and they are us!   One of the cruelest acts we could commit is to label something we do not understand as demonic.   We place ourselves at risk when we condemn an artwork we have never seen, or condemn an artist whose art we have not encountered.

Christ chose to hang out with the scum of the earth, the tax collectors, the harlots and the poor fishermen, because he knew these human individuals were not scum.   He only labeled those whom he *did* understand: the scribes, Pharisees and others who had raised the barrier of the law to keep themselves "pure."

Evil often wears the mask of purity.   This is the case in our culture as well.   "Art for art's sake" is the slogan of those who have attempted to rise above the common herd.   It is the battle cry of those who wish to separate themselves from the ignorant or the bourgeoisie.   But is it the battle cry of all artists?   It may be for some.   Clive Bell suggested: "To appreciate a work of art we need bring nothing with us but a sense of form and colour and a knowledge of three dimensional space."[6]

Such a reductionist approach to aesthetics was central to the art criticism of leading critics like Clement Greenberg: "Content is to be dissolved so completely into form that the work of art or literature cannot be reduced in whole or in part to anything but itself."[7] He made this assertion in spite of the rejection of his aesthetic by the very artists about whose work he wrote.   Clearly Rothko and Gottlieb did not see their work as purely self-referential when they wrote: "We assert that the subject is crucial and only that subject-matter is valid which is tragic and timeless.   That is why we profess spiritual kinship with primitive and archaic art."[8]   Their emphasis on subject matter is at odds with Greenberg's idea of pure painting as self-referential.   The archaic and primitive art Rothko and Gottlieb claim kinship with certainly referred to events, ideas and beliefs that were external to the art objects and their interior formal relationships.

Did the communication between artist and critic and public fail in part because the critics would not listen to the artists? Did Greenberg allow his theory to devour him, making it impossible for him to see the artworks for which he had developed it? Were the artists also at fault? Did they fail to communicate their intentions and ideas clearly, in their art and in their words? Was there something in their approach to making art that had misled the critics, or were the painters unwilling to acknowledge that they might be communicating something other than what they intended?

What role did the art-viewing public play? Did some accept this new art rather than be labeled *philistines*? And did other viewers merely reject these artworks out of hand, without attempting to engage in any real dialogue? Given the fallible nature of men and women, we can conclude that the breakdown in communication can be laid at the feet of all parties.

There are real demons and false demons. We will not uncover the false demons, nor rid ourselves of the real ones either, by shouting derisively at each other, through our journals and other publications. Nor will we do so by turning our backs and stiffening our necks rather than by painting or sculpting or weaving or writing or speaking to each other with respect, and in return seeing or reading or listening while making every effort to understand.

We only isolate ourselves when we refuse to communicate. The isolation that the refusal to communicate and receive communication constructs is the isolation of the omnipotent pretender. Since God is present in each person to whom we speak and to whom we listen, we place ourselves above God and reject God by refusing to participate in communication. And demons become demons by rejecting God.

Notes

1. H. R. Rookmaaker, *Modern Art & the Death of Culture* (Downers Grove, Illinois: Inter-Varsity Press, 1978), 130.

2. Diane Apostolos-Cappadona, "Dreams and Visions: Religious Symbols and Contemporary Culture," *Religion and Intellectual Life* (Spring 1984): 101.

3. Rookmaaker, 126.

4. Apostolos-Cappadona, 101.

5. Rookmaaker, 157.

6. Clive Bell, "Art as Significant Form: The Aesthetic Hypothesis," *Aesthetics: A Critical Anthology,* ed. by. George Dickie and Richard Sclafani (New York: St. Martin's Press, 1977), 44.

7. Clement Greenberg, *Art and Culture: Critical Essays* (Boston: Beacon Press: 1961), 5.

8. James E. B. Breslin, *Mark Rothko: A Biography* (Chicago: The University of Chicago Press, 1993), 193-94.

Essay 11

Quality

More than ordinary men or women, the significant painter, sculptor, musician or poet relates the raw material, the anarchic prodigalities of consciousness and sub-consciousness to the latencies, often unperceived, untapped before him, of articulation. This translation out of the inarticulate and the private into the general matter of human recognition requires the utmost crystalization and investment of introspection and control.[1]

George Steiner

Excellence, quality and achievement are terms that are endemic in our culture. We are constantly called to evaluate ourselves, to strive to better ourselves. Our colleagues admonish us: Dig deeper--try to make or do or envision what will enrich, improve or fulfill the high standards of our age. But why, and to what end?

That is the question. Many possible ends, including economic comfort or a place in history or self-expression, are valid and worthwhile. But are any of these sufficient? Or are there other more important motivations for artists to search, to work and think deeply, and to find ways to articulate visually what they can imagine or envision?

Yes, there are. Looking after our economic well being, making historically relevant art, expressing individual insights visually and articulating what we think can serve human culture. But none of these goals precludes making art of the sort Steiner describes. For him, it takes an extraordinary endeavor to create "true art." "True art" is outside of the ordinary.

Can we agree with Steiner? Can we always see the difference between the ordinary and the extraordinary? I believe it is harder than we think. For it is often in the ordinary object and through the everyday event that we are brought into the presence of the extraordinary, even miraculous--while on the other hand, what is clearly extraordinary in cost or size or human effort may end up leaving us cold and disappointed.

How each of us responds to the ordinary or the extraordinary is in the end subjective.   Thus, ordinary artifacts may or may not articulate feelings or concepts in ways that lift us out of the mundane.   They may not call us to think anew or feel anew; they may not have the capacity to transform us in any significant way although they decorate or ornament our environment and serve us well to that end.

Other ordinary artifacts--a pendant or ring--may illustrate or symbolize meaningful concepts, but not lead to insight.   Still other ordinary artifacts—a polished stone or worn piece of wood--may bring us great joy and delight, or remind us of the delicacy, complexity and wonder of the universe that surrounds us.   We may be brought anew to the realization of how extraordinary life itself is.   So what is ordinary may not be of poor quality; indeed it may be rich and revitalizing.

How does this relate to quality?   Often we are led to believe that the ordinary, because it is ordinary, cannot be of high quality.   But is this really the case?   Quality has been used to describe almost everything from used cars to the best we have to offer in the way of music or literature.   In reality, it does not necessarily imply valuation, though the term is often used as though it does.   Everything has many qualities--physical, formal, spiritual, intellectual.   With very few exceptions all of these qualities in a particular object or artwork are neither positive nor negative.   Instead, positive and negative are mingled.   So when an art object has many positive qualities and few negative qualities, it is considered to be of high quality.   The opposite, of course, may also be the case.   Ordinary objects, like all objects, may have predominantly positive or negative qualities.

But an ordinary object, such as a bowl, when perfection of utility is combined with formal, physical, intellectual and spiritual appropriateness, can rise above the typical plastic or ceramic bowl. One may be heavy and clunky; another may be too slippery to be held comfortably, while another may be ornamented in an unpleasant way. A bowl may be solid without being clunky, smooth without being slippery, and provide visual delight as well.   Both bowls are ordinary in function, but the second bowl provides a quality of satisfaction that the first does not.

The same may be true of a painting.   One image of a Madonna and Child may seem stiff, cool and overly ornamental.   Another may seem welcoming, warm and suitably complex in detail. Madonna and Child paintings make use of a typical subject. But the second may combine those qualities that are particularly appropriate for the image, and the meaning behind the image, in a way that makes the ordinary subject more inviting and effective.

So a clunky bowl and a cool Madonna may create the ordinary in a way that makes us wish to avoid rather than partake of them, while the visually delightful bowl and the warm Madonna invite. When we are delighted or warmly invited, we see or feel or think anew about that which is not new, for bowls and Madonna and Child images are not extraordinary at all. Whenever an artist makes a pitcher or print or drawing that is infused with a new vision for the ordinary, the ordinary is redeemed.

So how do we as artists take the ordinary object or subject or concept and invite, prod or persuade those who confront it towards some new insight? It is not easy to redeem the ordinary, to create those artworks that would renew our lives. Though it is not possible to pinpoint any particular, surefire route, it may be possible to point to some of the cul-de-sacs to avoid.

Excellence for the sake of excellence is one such. It is the route of the obsessive. It is the path of the perfectionist who would rid herself of all human imperfection in order to become superhuman. However, as Christians that is not our goal; we are called instead to become fully human. We are called to come to terms with our imperfections of body, mind and spirit, but not so that we dissect ourselves unto deathly perfection. Instead we are called to acknowledge our imperfections so that we might recognize that we are made complete only through Christ, not through our own efforts.

Once the false goal of perfection is recognized, then the goal of completion may take its place. But what does this have to do with the artist making art?

It is when the artist is aware that completion comes from God, not self, that redemption of the ordinary becomes possible. For God, a present but transcendent being who created all that is, is not ordinary. When the artist is aware, but not necessarily conscious, of what transcends the ordinary, she may be able to dwell within the realm of redemption long enough to draw from it some kernel of transcendence for her art. Through art this kernel can provide a glimmer of the wholeness that is possible with God. If seeking to proffer a glimmer of wholeness through art leads to excellence, then it is not excellence for its own sake.

Another cul-de-sac for artists is sincerity. That is a wonderful mindset, but it is never sufficient in itself. Sincere artists have produced truckloads of kitsch depicting the sentimental and the pious; the results are those banal and didactic visual sermons that no longer breathe life into anything. Sincerity is not a substitute for skill and passion, for thought and intuition. So sincerity divested of emotions, conceptual dexterity and formal daring is mind numbing, life draining and spirit dampening.

Yet insincerity is even worse, for in connection to art, it means the artist sees his viewers as marionettes. So his art simulates the strings that manipulate the limbs, lips and head. Making viewers who can be jerked about at will is the vocation of a sadist, not an artist. Sincerity has a place in art, but unaccompanied by emotional, spiritual and intellectual awareness and highly developed skills, it spawns only kitsch.

The use of significant subjects and meaningful symbols in art does not guarantee artworks that are kitsch-proof. As our greeting card industry has ably demonstrated, any subject, be it a crucifixion or an annunciation, can be drained of impact and diluted to the point of insignificance. Transforming significant events, impassioned feelings or noble thoughts into vapid visual compositions is a sad and graceless form of duplicity. Artists who make the extraordinary appear ordinary do a disservice both to their compositions and art.

Quality and excellence--the ability to make objects that embody redemption--are rarer than our culture likes to believe. Advertisers tout the excellence of their products. Artists often follow the same path. Balancing between hyper-humility and egotism is difficult to attain and maintain.

Finding this balance is further complicated when Christians receive confusing messages from their leaders, writers, and educators. On the one hand, we are told each of us is special in God's eyes. And this is true. Yet we often forget our special-ness is not a result of our own merit. On the other hand, we are told we are grievous sinners. And this is also true. Then we forget we are God-beloved in spite of our sinfulness. How are we to hold fast to the realization that each of us is badly flawed but greatly loved? There is no easy answer. And this is fortunate. For if the answer were too easily found, we would cease searching, each of us, for our path to completion and wholeness in God.

What is even more confusing is that Christian leaders sometimes tell us that our faith will make us rich and successful and powerful, while they forget to remind us that our riches and our success and our power will be unlike what this world values.   Sifting wheat from chaff is a recurring challenge.

An artist whose art reflects his search for wholeness in God will not purposely lie to us; such art will shy away from both egotistical self-congratulation and false humility.   Quality or excellence may be present in such art because it reflects transcendent reality.   And because the artist is making a diligent attempt to realize that wholeness for humans comes through brokenness and imperfection rather than some utopian vision of humanly attainable perfection, her artwork may reach beyond the ordinary.

Notes

1. George Steiner, *Real Presences* (Chicago: The University of Chicago Press, 1989), 12.

Essay 12

Spirit

Our sacramental "mindset" has taken on many of the characteristics of
our post-Industrial, consumerist society. In this society, the beautiful
has become the pretty, goodness has become duty, and truth has become
the verification of data. Our lives have been flattened and our symbolic
expression has become yet another sub-language.[1]

Susan A. Ross

Spirituality is linked with so many concepts, acts and experiences
that seem at odds with each other. As a result we don't have a clear
idea of what we mean when the term *spiritual* is linked with art.
Spirituality, in the recent past, has often been linked with what is
transcendent. But the term *transcendent* does not do much to clarify
issues of spirituality.

In the twentieth century artists often strove to create art that referred
only to itself, or on the other hand, made art that enabled the viewer to
transcend self either through an emotional or intellectual experience.
Art that refers only to itself is intentionally objective, non-
representational, non-transcendent. At least this is what we are led to
believe. However, such art is not merely self-referential. By
implication, self-referential art places value on objective reality alone.
Such art denies or devalues transcendence. It is based upon verifiable
visual data reflecting objective reality, while not representing it. Does
this mean that self-referential art cannot be metaphorical? Does it not,
by analogy, symbolize an objectivist mindset? I will leave the
answering of these questions to those who make and explain self-
referential art.

Transcendent art, on the other hand, seeks to enlarge the viewer's
experience of reality with symbols or evocative imagery. It is intended

to encourage humanity to fullness, as opposed to the flatness Ross describes above.

Makers of transcendent art usually want us to become transformed into participants. Makers of self-referential art, on the other hand, do not encourage participation beyond factual verification of visual, spatial or conceptual data input.

When contemplating self-referential art, one remains an observer always able to separate the observing self from the observed artwork. The opposite is intended for viewers of transcendent art. For once the viewers become participants, objectivity is no longer possible. Or as Ross puts it:

> [I]t can be argued that the work of art is by its nature designed to draw the experiencer into its own world. To be caught up in a work of art is to leave (at least temporarily) one's ordinary world and to experience an alternative world.[2]

For many artists, art historians and art critics, art that encourages or invites participation and transcendence is called spiritual. Often the use of *spiritual* in relation to this art implies no connection with religion or faith. The spirit referred to is the human spirit. Such spirituality is about transcending the individual self in order to experience communion either with humanity or the natural world.

Artists who imbue their artwork with human spirituality invite others to participate with them in a fuller experiential understanding of what human life in the natural world is about. This is good, for invigorating our lives through experience fills us and lifts us from the flatness of the mundane.

Clearly the limitations of human spirituality are not sufficient for some artists. They invite us to transcend our human limitations--in order to experience something greater than humanity or the natural world of physical sensations. They want to bring us into contact with some Jungian (or other) version of the subconscious psychic undercurrent that informs our present conscious existence.

Or they may want us to transcend the limitations of our culture and time so that we might experience something outside of what we know. This can also bring us insight into other ways of seeing and experiencing human existence.

Another level of spirituality is informed by a belief in sacredness. Sacred means to be "set apart or dedicated to some religious purpose."[3] And art can point to what is sacred or set apart because it may transcend a particular time or place, and direct us towards gods or God.

This type of spirituality has been the goal of artists for most of human existence. It is only in the last few centuries that "spiritual" subjects, symbols and images have not dominated art. The purpose of "spiritual" or sacred art is to lead us to participate more fully in religious life and to experience more deeply the divine.

However, using spirituality to refer to art specifically related to religious belief or experience can be confusing. Because, for some, all of creation is imbued with the spiritual. In effect then there is no such thing as the secular. For God encompasses all that is or informs through creation all that is, thus making everything spiritual in the third sense of the term as discussed above. It is possible, from a Christian point of view, to assert that since God is within us, every moment becomes a holy moment filled with spirituality whether or not we are attending to God's presence in that moment.

Yes, but what about art that seems to deny God or ignores God? Is that spiritual too? In the negative sense yes. For all spirituality is not good or godly spirituality. Artists can intentionally negate God and or the natural world through their art. In other words they can make art that asserts an anti-creative spirituality.

However art, which involves the making of things or the contemplation of concepts (even negative concepts), is *per se* a creative stance that reflects a positive or pro-creative approach to life. For to be truly anti-creative art must be actively destructive, not just make use of anti-creative imagery or concepts. Even nihilists betray themselves as less than true nihilists if they actively advocate nihilism. A true nihilist would make no such effort, for there would be no purpose to be served by such advocacy in a universe in which nothing has purpose.

So, in a universe created by God, it is difficult to make art that is not in some way spiritual. This does not mean that some artworks are not more "spiritual" in the deepest sense of that word. If the intention is shallow, or the execution is flawed, or the concept is presented poorly, the spiritual effect will be hindered.

Spirituality is not necessarily dependent upon the type of subject or the conceptual approach or content. A still life may be more spiritually evocative than a crucifixion. It all depends upon the skills and conceptual abilities of the artist. A devout Christian artist will not necessarily paint or sculpt more deeply spiritual artworks that an agnostic artist. However, this does not mean that there is no value in painting crucifixions or in an artist's being a Christian. It merely means that depth of Christian belief and the use of Christian imagery do not guarantee spiritually effective and affective artworks.

Even if an artwork is found to be deeply spiritual, it does not mean that all who see it will be drawn to participate in this spirituality. For the artwork is not itself a spiritual object. The artwork may be the catalyst for a spiritual experience. It may be designed and executed by the artist with the intention and hope that a spiritual experience will result. But the spirit can only dwell in what is living. An artist cannot transform clay or paint or ink into a place of spiritual indwelling.

An artist can, however, use clay or paint or ink to create a stage on which spiritual dance may take place. The way the artwork is conceived and executed can at best invite the viewer to participate, to dance with the Holy Spirit, who is everywhere present. It does not reflect poorly on the artist maker or the viewer who sees but does not find the spiritual in every artwork. For each of us has been made differently and each of us will respond to different invitations from the Holy Spirit.

Fortunately the Holy Spirit is gracious and will keep inviting us through art, and many other means, to dance, to play, to dwell in this seemingly evanescent realm that is as solid and real as anything our senses can grasp. Artists cannot make artworks spiritual or sacred or holy. Artworks themselves are not spiritual or sacred or holy, but they may act as pathways, windows or invitations that invite us to participate with what is spiritual, sacred or holy.

How does the artist work towards creating these invitations to spiritual participation? There is no set of rules, precepts or principles for the artist to follow. But an artist might find some things helpful. Prayer is always a place to start. Since its intention is to connect us with God's spirituality, it can deepen the spiritual life of the artist. The artist cannot pray his way into producing spirituality effective art, but prayer can lead to a deeper experience of God's holiness.

Another path is to reflect on those artworks or experiences that have invited you to participate in spiritual dance or holy play. Ask yourself questions about what you respond to in artworks or experiences, and then why. What kinds of thoughts and feelings emerge from these experiences, and what elicits these thoughts and feelings?

Yet another way to understand pathways to the spiritual is to study your audiences--take on the role of an involved (not detached) observer. Creating art is not a one-way street. If an artwork is to act as invitation, or even as an effective confrontation, it cannot be made in a vacuum. Perhaps the first step is to cease thinking of the people out there as an audience. The term audience implies a one-way communication with the artist as active maker or giver and audience as passive receivers of art.

To make effective and inviting windows or entrances, the artist needs an understanding that comes from awareness. Focusing on, attending to, and not just superficially, the needs, wants and desires of others can help the artist craft his work in a way that is diligent and loving.

Art created by the diligent and loving artist may not always please each individual who sees the artwork. On the other hand, it does not preclude pleasing those individuals. Prayer, an understanding of what invites or prods us towards the spiritual and a respect for those who respond to an artwork may help artists make art that leads toward a greater awareness of God's spirit of acceptance and God's invitation to spiritual communion.

Notes

1. Susan A. Ross, "The Aesthetic and the Sacramental," *Worship* (January 1985): 16.

2. Ross, 4.

3. *The Compact Edition of the Oxford English Dictionary* (Oxford: Oxford University Press, 1971), II, 2616.

Essay 13

Words

> If we have allowed theology to become almost exclusively a theology
> of the Word we need to re-read both Genesis I and the Prologue to St.
> John's gospel to remind ourselves that the primal Word is itself the
> bringing into being of light, the light which is the ground-stuff of
> creation and of human consciousness.   Nor is this the light some kind
> of hidden inner quality.   It is radiance, the spatialization of being,
> significant form, structuring the world in such a way as to make it see-
> able, and the condition of all subsequent meaning and all subsequent
> logos elements, including the logos of theology.[1]

George Pattison

"Since its inception, Protestantism has been charmed by the printing
press."[2] Parker writes.   Roman Catholicism, though it has suffered the
visual arts to play a wider role, has also been entranced by the written
and printed word.

As we said much of this honoring of the spoken, written and later the
printed word comes from a fear of creating graven images.   And
creating images that might be taken as substitutes for the real thing was
a problem for the peoples we read about in the Bible.   It will always
remain a problem.   But the Church has not forbidden speech even
though there are numerous Biblical examples of people giving verbal
false witness, telling lies and making self-serving false prophecies.   As
Jay C. Rochelle points out, idolatry is not limited to visual images and
artifacts:

> "To have no graven images" means that no concepts, doctrines, mental
> sets, or cultural patterns are allowed to block the free flow of the
> visionary process.   The attempt to make a plastic or verbal work of art
> is not against the spirit of the commandment so long as the thing made

remains a message/icon pointing beyond itself, transparent to the power of Life itself in creation.[3]

Thus discarding or downgrading the visual in preference to the verbal is to miss the point about idolatry.

So idolatry is not the most significant issue, it is a diversion that keeps us from the central issue, which is, for our culture and the Church, our fear of fact.   In spite of the fact that the WORD did not remain word, that the WORD became physically, tangibly en-fleshed, the Church has been and remains uncomfortable with the visual because it is fact.   This discomfort with what is en-fleshed is not unique to the Church.   Much of the contemporary unease with allowing the visual to play a significant role in Christian life comes from other sources.

Our intellectual culture is largely to blame.   As mentioned previously, it is dominated by the written word.   As a culture we have become more comfortable with abstraction, verbally or mathematically formulated, than with factual reality.   Verbal abstractions are much more tractable, flexible and susceptible to gymnastic interpretation. The object with all its stubborn and concrete there-ness confronts us so definitely with its particularity that we can not avoid or evade it without some difficulty.

As a culture we prefer commentary or statistical analysis to the actual fact.   For commentary and statistical analysis can always be teased or tweaked, re-evaluated and re-worked.   The object, including the art object, remains stubbornly there, intruding into our awareness whether or not it is convenient.

Perhaps the uncomfortable nature of fact is the reason no major intellectual journal publishes reproductions of visual artifacts accompanied only with the necessary labels.   We have become verbally dependent and visually impaired as a society.

Even art museums feel compelled to print catalogues and provide a recorded dialogue for viewers.   As a culture we can no longer allow a visual artwork to stand alone to speak for itself, unaccompanied by a verbal translation.   Unfortunately, as long as churches, universities and museums are dominated by men and women of letters this is not likely to change significantly.   It does not mean we should abandon attempts to open our culture to the value of the visual arts.

In Christian institutions the visual arts are often looked upon with suspicion because artists are too independent minded and too unpredictable, and they make things that we don't always understand or that make us uncomfortable.   Christian institutions, above all, fear embarrassment: "Witness the miniscule size of the art department at any Christian college. With the exception of the music conservatory, the arts are restricted to an inconspicuous cranny, lest any would-be contributor stumble upon some naked Venus."[4]

However, by banishing, severely circumscribing or minimizing the visual arts, Christian bodies risk blindness. As Robert F. McGovern avers: "The artist must honor both the needs that others have for beauty and their ways of expressing these needs. The public must start to trust the soundless voice of art. Our fate is collective."[5] Like one of the three monkeys we may hide our eyes behind our hands so that we will see no evil. But then we can also see no good. Our very souls may be dependent upon being willing to see what is evil so that we may also see what is good.

It is clear that the Bible provides examples of God calling upon the people of Israel to make artifacts that we would call art. In the Old Testament God called for the construction of the Temple in Jerusalem, the Ark of the Covenant and the Brazen Serpent. On the other hand, the New Testament does not speak often or directly about the visual arts. The City of God described briefly in Revelation is the most concrete example.

However, the role of the artist by analogy may also be present in the story of the woman who washes Jesus' feet. How? This woman performs a beautiful and extravagant act, extravagant because she uses an expensive ointment. But more importantly because she does it with her whole self, without reserve. Simon the Pharisee, representing respectable society, is repulsed by the impropriety and intimacy of this act.[6] In a similar manner an artist pours herself out, using oil paints, bronze, and other costly materials into a most intimate and revealing action that results in an art object. This object, because of its intimate nature, often makes the socially respectable uncomfortable. The significant part of the story about the woman who washes Jesus' feet is the fact of Jesus' acceptance of both the woman and her action.

Yet the most convincing claim of the visual arts in the New Testament is Jesus himself. Once God created humans he knew that humanity would not come to true belief without experiential evidence of himself. Thus God, as perfect creator-imager, created a self-portrait of the Godhead in Jesus. Jesus is made in the image of God. He is the perfect visual embodiment of God, creator and maker of all.

Instead of communicating through abstractions alone, as represented by the Ten Commandments, God allowed humanity to directly experience godly perfection in living, visual form. Jesus' life was a preordained, but unscripted, performance piece. He spoke unscripted words and was the WORD too--but not word alone, he was also a visual and physical embodiment.

What was important about this visual and physical embodiment was not so much its gender, which was male (since in Christ there is no male or female), but its moral, ethical and spiritual perfection. It is also significant that Jesus, as the embodiment of God, was not merely a preacher and a social reformer. He was much more. Jesus was a person who celebrated God's living creation through feasts, quiet times in a garden, storytelling sessions and attending to children, the sick and the downtrodden.

This self-portrait that God chose to paint was not that of a grim and sour but dutiful individual. His self-portrait image is filled with insight and tenderness. Christ's physical sensitivity was so great that he knew instantly when he was touched by a sick woman, whom he praised for her faith (Lk 8:43-48). He exhibited both insight and tenderness in his interactions with the Samaritan woman at the well (Jn 4:7-30). He responded with wit and intelligence when he replied to the Pharisees who had come to trap him by referring to a Roman coin (Mk 12:13-17). Anger and resolute action was his response to the moneychangers in the temple (Jn 2:13-22).

God's self-portrait is not a simple one-dimensional illustration without depth and complexity. It is a fully fleshed-out image of moral, ethical and spiritual perfection in human form. And not coincidentally this fleshed-out human form worked with his hands. Christ was not merely an intellectual concerned with abstractions, theses and theoretical propositions. He was concerned with the reality of the present moment and how those he cared for (which includes all humans) were affected by whatever was occurring in that present moment. Words alone were not deemed by God to be sufficient for his self-revelation.

Notes

1. George Pattison, "Art and Apologetics," *Modern Churchman* 32 (1991): 29.

2. Peggy Parker, "A Journey of Discovery," *ARTS: The Arts in Religious and Theological Studies* (Summer 1993): 14.

3. Jay C. Rochelle, "Proclamation and Vision," *Dialog* (Spring 1981): 94.

4. Ken Bazin, "Reclaiming the Arts," *ACTION* (Summer 1977): 12.

5. Robert F. McGovern, "A Re-emergence of Religious Art in the Seventies," *Dimension* (Summer 1974): 90.

6. Douglas Campbell, "The Role of Art," *Voices in the Wilderness* (March/April 1988): 10-12.

Essay 14

Originality

The Genius of the artist finds its way by the affinity of creative sympathy, or conaturality, into the living law that rules the universe. This law is nothing but the secret gravitation that draws all things to God as to their center.[1]

Thomas Merton

The fact that each of us is unique does not mean that what we make will be original, even if it is unique. Our culture is enamored with the news and the new. We cannot escape the barrage of news programs on radio and television. The Internet provides us with potentially endless hours of information-gathering twenty-four hours a day. News reporters are constantly scouring the earth for something new to report.

Actually they are not so much interested in the new, but would much prefer to find the sensational, the disastrous or the bizarre. Our eyes and ears are filled with warnings of new viruses, economic downturns, child abuse, weather-related disasters and other threats to our lives. We either isolate ourselves from the news or we become desensitized to a deluge of reports about bombings, multiple car accidents, earthquakes and terrorist attacks. We begin to believe that nothing exists but chaos.

Culture is a supposed antidote to the fragmented world that surrounds us. Traditionally culture provided stability, helped us to know who we were and helped us understand how to relate to each other and the natural world. Yet for centuries our cultural citadels have been crumbling, and the new cultural paradigms, though intellectually stimulating, have not created a stable base upon which we can stand securely.

Even the most cursory look through a general history of art text makes it clear that change, not stability, is the rule, not an exception. As we move into the twenty-first century, we find ourselves awash, flooded with competing stylistic and conceptual approaches to art, many at odds with each other. As discussed previously, part of our confusion is no doubt the result of the idea of the "mainstream" in the history of art. This has indoctrinated us with a false vision of the past, a vision that smoothed over the rough places, ignored what did not fit and concerned itself primarily with Western art by men, because this simplified the study of art.

An unfortunate result of this "mainstream" model is that it presents a much simpler vision of the past than the one that truly occurred. So when we confront the diversity surrounding us today, we are at a loss to know how to cope with it, for it does not fit our simplistic model. Once we understand that change and confusing diversity are normative for human cultures, then we can begin to look at our own artistic culture with less fear.

What is different about our culture is that the media make us constantly aware of these changes and this diversity more rapidly, even incessantly. What would take years, months or weeks to travel from one town or nation to another is now transferred almost instantaneously. We may more easily despair of being able to deal with all that is there to digest, accept or reject. Our media-dominated society more often than not presents an image of our world that resembles a vast nursery for infants, filled with a cacophony of unintelligible voices crying out for attention.

To be noticed has become our cultural objective. And to be noticed we have learned we must do something mighty. It really doesn't matter so much what is done as long as the doing of it is loud and shrill. The world of art is not immune to our societal and cultural practices: artists are encouraged to focus on some unique stylistic approach, conceptual approach or materials as means to the creation of something "new" (meaning unique).

Unfortunately the word *original* is now used as if it were synonymous with *unique*. Unique means only different, and traditionally no value was necessarily added to an object or event so labeled. Original has come to encompass different, but means more—it now implies that the object or idea so labeled is valued because it provides newness, or because it provides a heightened experience, a unique insight or a divergent conceptual framework.

But is it ultimately valid, and therefore valuable? In other words, what is the value this art enfolds--experience to what end, insight into what, conceptual framework for what? If the answer is experience of deep acceptance, insight into what love is, or a conceptual framework for improving the relationship between humankind and nature, then we might say that this originality has value. On the other hand if the experience is of deep and thrilling vengeance, or insight into some newly available narcotic bliss, or a conceptual framework for justifying germ warfare, then we might be inclined to say that such originality has little value. Is there a better way to think about the word *originality*?

For Christians true originality is not about being unique or different. Instead, the word itself tells us it is about origins or sources. So for Christians to be original means to be directed towards the source or origin of all that is. Instead of pridefully seeking to be idiosyncratically unique, a Christian artist might humbly seek through his art to direct the viewers' attention towards God, the origin and source of all that is true, beautiful or valuable.

This does not imply that a unique approach may not be an original approach. Sometimes it provides a new path towards God. The difference between this type of God-directed originality and "originality," as used in common parlance, is that the latter may or may not lead towards something of value, while the former always does. For artists, seeking to be original is a mistake, for as created beings we cannot be original on our own.

"Originality for originality's sake" cannot lead to a good artwork. Instead the artist would do better to open herself to where her feelings or spirit or mind is leading her. If an artist has the requisite skills, then something of the original may come out of the art-making process. Although there is no model to follow that will insure originality. Christians may find that meditation or reading the Bible and other books (either overt or otherwise in their spiritual guise), looking at works of art, talking with friends or praying will help them. There is no predicting when we might be struck with an insight that may bring about an original artwork.

But what if I (the artist) don't create anything original, will I then have failed? Perhaps in the eyes of the art historians I will have failed to rise to the category of genius. But that is the case for almost everyone. Few women or men ever do or make anything reflective of the original in the grand sense. But then I have not yet found in the Bible that we are admonished "to look upon the originality of God, and do likewise with all of our mind and heart and will."

Only those confused about the role of humans on earth would desire such a preposterous calling. May our desire be instead to please God by creating original artworks that will draw others closer to him. Are we afraid that God will not accept us if we are not able to make a painting, print, ceramic piece or video that does not thrill the art historians, museum curators and the public? This is not the case, for God's love is not contingent. In fact we would all be better off if we would forget about being original in any sense of the term, and instead focus on being open to God, to where God is leading us in this frustrating, humbling and exciting journey called life.

We are more likely to do something original (in relation to art) if our focus is God rather our places in the history or art. Our openness to God may take us places we never expected to go, may draw forth from us art that is surprising and vital and healing--perhaps something original.

Notes

1. Thomas Merton, *No Man Is an Island* (New York: Harcourt Brace Jovanovich, 1955), 36.

Essay 15

Theory

Freud and Sophocles are at opposite poles of our life's spectrum: one explains order by a model, the other creates an order by shaping a space of his own. If the theory saves me from chaos, art saves me from theory.[1]

Samuel Laeuchli

Perhaps the trinity is the best model for Christians of how good art functions. The trinity is composed of three parts: 1. creator (the maker of new things), 2. son (the embodiment of creation), and 3. Holy Spirit (the giver of insight--literally providing us the sight to see within ourselves so that we know about the lack of and presence of truth therein). The unified Trinity is nevertheless divided into three separate parts. But these persons are in constant communication. Art then strives to become a dialogue or trialogue modeled on these communicating, interacting parts of God.[2]

The absence of any of these three elements leads to stillbirth and failure. At times the brilliance of the creative force behind the work may overwhelm us. At times the physical presence of the artwork may overload our mental or emotional circuits. Or at times we may feel filled with insight that allows us to see beyond the surface of the artwork down into the truth that it may hold. No artwork is a perfect balance of these three distinct parts, for, as has been said, only God can produce such perfection.

Even though Christian artists will never attain perfect balance, it is possible to strive for balance. If the artist seeks to be creative, to use his God-given imaginative capacity, then his art can exhibit some glimpse of God's imagination. The artist can make the invisible visible if she works to acquire skill and sensitivity to her materials and media.   If the artist is open to the spirit of God present in all things, then her art can be true both to its maker and media and thus allow the viewer the experiences of God-informed insight.   When the artist is able to do all three things in her work, then there is a balance of the self (the creator), the created object (the media) and the spiritual (the giver of insight).

It should be clear that creative gifts are not self-given.   Even the secular arena uses the terms *talented* and *gifted* to label those who have exceptional skill and the ability to use them creatively.   All artists, whether Christian or not, derive their creative gifts or powers from God.   Like any other gifts the individual who has them can choose to use them.   They can be used to enhance the self, to search for truth, to create something that can delight or entertain, or to degrade both the artist and the viewer.

Since no artist is able to discern the truth in all instances, no artist can image the perfect reflection of truth.   For the Christian artist the best goal may be to image pieces of the truth (like pieces in an immense jigsaw puzzle).   Each artist provides a fragment of the truth. So those who view these fragments through the works of many artists and consider these individual images (or puzzle pieces)--can experience visions of truth more fully than they might without visual images. Artists are not the only ones with imaginations or means of embodying the fruits of the imagination.   However they do have a particularly powerful means of imaging truth.

Image without embodiment is certainly possible.   However, embodiment communicates effectively.   Since we are physical beings, much of our understanding of the world about us is based on the physical and tangible and on our experience of the sensations they engender.   Thus there is a valid place for those objects that embody the creative imaginations of the artist.

Our reactions and sensations resulting from confronting or contemplating artworks will not be uniform.   For one thing our bodies are not uniform; that is why each of us responds differently to each object we confront.   Yet, even though our bodies may differ, they also have much in common.   So there is also similarity in our responses to objects (a sharp knife will cut your finger whether you are tall or short). Our physical difference is mirrored by our emotional difference.   Since our life experiences and organic predispositions are not uniform, we will have disparate emotional reactions to objects.   Our intellectual responses reflect divergent intellectual paths.   And our spiritual responses will be diverse, for our spiritual pilgrimages have led each of us to follow our own footsteps crossing deserts, following the wide highway or the "road less traveled."

An art object, no matter how significant the artist's image, no matter how finely crafted, will attract little note if it does not offer insight for at least some of those individual viewers who try understand. So to be valued as art, as opposed to a collection of materials, each effective artwork's maker seeks to provide a doorway for insight to pass through.

Clearly insight cannot enter an artist or a viewer who is not receptive. And no theory or set of principles will provide a skeleton key that will unlock all possible doors to creative insight--each theory may unlock a variety of doors, but none yet found will unlock all. So each time an artist opens herself to God's insight, she may open a new door or add new road to the map. Whether this artwork, this a new passage, will allow insight to pass through it is dependent upon how the artist responds to the creative moment. A theory may bring the artist to this moment, but theory alone cannot redeem it.

Though a Trinitarian model for thinking about art may help the artist to understand how an artwork might possibly work, it does not provide any distinct guidelines for the artist to follow. There is no set of rules, no process, no conceptual framework, no method of emotional, spiritual or intellectual preparation that will ensure the making of good or effective art. As Laeuchli suggests, art saves us from theory, theory that would limit freedom and perpetuate bondage.

Twentieth century art swung like a pendulum from theory-based art to anti-theoretical art. Neoplasticism, Minimalism, Cubism, Constructivism, Purism, Suprematism, Conceptualism and others represent theoretical approaches. And German Expressionism, Abstract Expressionism, Dadaism, Surrealism, Neoexpressionism and others represent anti-theoretical approaches. The amazing result is that art from each of these styles has provided intellectual insights or deep spiritual probing or emotional experiences that transcended the theory or the lack of theory.

On the other hand much produced under these stylistic banners has resulted in artwork that seems needlessly redundant. To ignore theory, principles or processes is to court chaos filled with warped, conceited and toxic mutations. To worship theory and follow it religiously is to build what is hollow and sterile, unfit for living humans. Both paths are pride-filled. Anti-theoretical approaches assert the omnipotence of the artist, placing him above all accumulated bodies of knowledge and making him an independent genius. Theoretical approaches also assert the omnipotence of the artist, assuming that all knowledge can be mastered by an individual or small group of individuals.

The author of Ecclesiastes bemoans such pretensions when he writes, "Vanity of vanities, says the Teacher, vanity of vanities! All is vanity" (Eccl 1:2). The calling of the artist is not to place himself God-like upon a pedestal, nor to construct theoretical towers that will eventually tumble down upon the innocent. Perhaps the real artistic genius, though not always recognized as such, is the artist who can make art that gives the viewer intellectual, emotional or spiritual insight while remaining authentically humble. Economic, cultural, social, emotional, psychological, intellectual and spiritual deficits are what stand in the way of authentic humility for the artist--or for that matter, for any of us.

Notes

1. Samuel Laeuchli, *Religion and Art in Conflict: Introduction to a Cross-Disciplinary Task* (Philadelphia: Fortress Press: 1980), 54.

2. For further study of the Trinity in relation to the arts refer to *The Mind of the Maker* by Dorothy Sayers. For a discussion of the Trinity in relation to a specific visual art refer to "Creator Creation and Creativity" by James Romaine in *It was Good, Making Art to the Glory of God.* For further discussion of interrelational aspects of the Trinity, refer to *God For Us: The Trinity and Christian Life* by Catherine Mowry LaCugna.

Essay 16

Stewardship

Art, like religious faith in general and prayer in particular, has the power to help us transcend the fragmented society we now inhabit. We live now in a Babel of antagonistic tribes--tribes that speak only the languages of race, class, rights, and ideology. That is why the intuitive language of the imagination is so vital. Reaching deep into our collective thoughts and memories, great art sneaks past our shallow prejudices and brittle opinions to remind us of the complexity and mystery of human existence.[1]

Gregory Wolfe

It is a truism that our culture is a disintegrated culture. Political parties, ethnic groups, numerous special interest groups thrust their agendas at each other as they raise their defenses high. The very fabric of our culture is constantly warped and rent by the struggles that conflicting agendas create.

In the midst of all this Christians are called to be stewards of the earth, to be reconcilers, to be healers who fashion wholeness where destruction is rampant. Often they have decided to enter the fray as combatants, to become one of the warring parties rather take on the role of peacemakers. Often Christians have chosen to condemn what they find abhorrent rather than lift up what they find life-giving. How do Christians and Christian artists work toward finding positive and healing approaches in this present cultural environment?

The answer to this question is both simple and complicated. One conceptually simple step would be to give up the language of combat. An example of the Christian battle cry is found in Sharon Porlier's article "The Trustee Nature of Christian Art." Porlier interprets Daniel, chapter 1, verse 32 as a call to war. She writes, "The second half of this verse gives us our life work, our battle plan."[2] Porlier interprets "but the people who know God shall be strong and do exploits" (Dn 11:32) to mean that they will engage in battle.

However the subsequent verse does not support this interpretation. Daniel chapter 11, verse 33 reads: "The wise among the people shall give understanding to many; for some days, however, they shall fall by the sword and flame, and suffer captivity and plunder." Wise women and men do not issue a call to battle though they may become victims of it.   Instead, they give understanding to the people and endure suffering or death.   To refuse combat is a simple but difficult choice--a choice that may bring attack from other Christians as well as non-Christians.

A more complicated and perhaps no less difficult answer to the question is to offer up a positive alternative to the art that is found to be lacking in truth or morality.   Though I may not wish to respond to Porlier's call to arms, I do agree with her when she writes: "Christian artists must have great strength which comes from knowing, having confidence in and obeying their God.   The sweet sentimentality commonly associated with Christian art simply will not do."[3]

It takes great strength to maintain integrity in a disintegrated cultural environment.   And sugarcoating the truth is no way to maintain integrity.   But each time an artist draws us into a particular artwork that leads us closer to understanding God, ourselves, our neighbors or our environment, we are drawn towards integration.   Offering a path towards integration or wholeness within a disintegrated world is both healing and reconciling.

Clearly no one path will be able to draw everyone towards wholeness.   Exceptional artworks, ones that may be labeled classics in the future, are precisely those works that have great power in drawing us in and then pointing the way towards integrity.   While not all artworks are great art, there are many that have the potential to bring healing and reconciliation--physical, emotional, spiritual and intellectual.   Christian artists who seek to be true to God's calling can play an important role in reintegrating individuals and communities. Even though our culture at large and the artists' own faith communities may ignore or dismiss artists, it does not mean that God has dismissed them.

Another means Christians have for drawing both Christians and non-Christians closer to the truth through art is to encourage artists to follow the path to which God has led them.   But how can this be done in the current contentious environment?   Gregory Wolfe has written:

It is my conviction that the Christian community, despite its many laudable efforts to preserve traditional mores and the social fabric, has abdicated its stewardship of culture and, more importantly, has substituted ideology for imagination in its approach to the crisis of our time.[4]

But rather than merely criticize the Christian community and leave it at that, Wolfe has created *Image*, a publication that showcases works of art that act to continue the Judeo-Christian tradition. Through it readers are presented with artworks by a variety of artists that may confront our complacency and comfort us in our suffering. *Image* has become a conduit connecting readers with artworks that they are not likely to find in any other publication. *ARTS: The Arts in Religious and Theological Studies* and *Christianity and the Arts* also encourage artists and help shape a Christian vision of an integrated culture.

Though publications provide an easily accessible means for visual communication, they are not necessarily the most effective means. Seeing actual artworks is better than seeing reproductions, though seeing reproductions is better than missing them altogether. Many organizations within the broader Christian community are providing exhibition opportunities for artists working with Christian imagery, subjects and content.

Christian colleges and universities have gallery spaces devoted at least in part to Christian imagery, subject and content. Juried exhibits that focus on Christian themes or imagery have become more numerous within the past decade or two.[5] These provide artists more chances to exhibit their artworks. A painting stored in the artist's closet or a sculpture stored in an artist's basement is merely another light under a basket.

Another positive step towards allowing the arts to bring healing and reconciliation to the battlefield of the "culture wars" is through Christian arts organizations. Christians in the Visual Arts (CIVA) is one of the largest and most active Christian arts organizations in this country. It is also an international organization sponsoring national and regional conferences where artists fellowship, listen to guest speakers and each other, participate in formal and informal discussions, and have an opportunity to show slides of their works or bring artworks for display. Christian artists from all over the United States and beyond can come together and be comforted and inspired. CIVA gives artists a chance to dismantle the isolation in which they often exist.

CIVA also makes available traveling exhibits, a slide reference library and a framework for a positive, imaginative and creative response to a fragmented world.   And artists who are Mennonite, Roman Catholic, Lutheran, Episcopalian, Greek Orthodox, Baptist, and those from many other denominations, or from independent Christian communities, are welcomed.

Local and regional Christian arts organizations perform a similar positive function.   The Christian Fine Arts Association, Denver, Colorado; Sanctuary for the Arts, Portland, Oregon; The Liturgical Arts Guild, Worthington, Ohio; and the New York Arts Group, New York City, function to meet the needs of their artist members.   Some of these organizations provide community acceptance for Christian artists where none existed, while others offer a wide range of services including exhibitions, workshops, and library resources.

Publications, exhibitions, workshops and conferences for Christian artists are steps towards redeeming culture.   They provide a positive alternative to the call to take part in ideological bloodletting or to engage in rancorous battle.   But as long as Christian artists remain immersed within this ghetto of faith, what they have to reveal through art will have little effect on culture at large.   They should be encouraged to step outside their own faith ghettos, encouraged to risk sharing their artworks in venues that draw upon the population at large.

There is no one right way to do this.   Each artist must discern what she or he is called to do, with and through art.   For some, entering juried exhibits outside the Christian orbit may be the answer.   For others, it may mean finding independent galleries to show their work.

As artists take steps to draw human culture towards God and God's truth, they can be assisted by Christian art critics and Christian art historians who are willing to write about this art for presses outside the Christian domain.   For as long as Christians talk only to each other, or write only for each other or make art only for each other, what they have to say or write or paint or engrave or carve or stitch will have only indirect impact.   If artists believe that what they form is true, then let it be seen.

Yet artists are not given total responsibility for redeeming culture. Institutions and organizations, those multi-human organisms so dominated by self-preservation, must be humanized.   Denominations, churches, Christian colleges and universities and other Christian organizations need to be transformed and "beat their swords into plowshares."   Leaders of these organizations must choose life, choose communication instead of diatribe.

Since each administrative decision reflects a cultural perspective, administrators cannot ignore the arts.   Instead of buying from a catalogue, contact an artist.   Instead of using posters that the publishing houses provide so cheaply, contact an artist.   Instead of adding art to a completed church building, invite artists to play a role in the planning process.   Take artists seriously as individuals who have a vital and important role to play.   Any organization that ignores the arts puts itself in grave danger of becoming inhumane.   For the arts, from the very beginning of human existence, have provided humanity with a means to transcend our human failings and find God, in spite of the many barriers that our warring human cultures have devised.

Notes

1. Gregory Wolfe, "Art, Faith, and the Stewardship of Culture," *Regeneration Quarterly* (Spring 1996): 18.

2. Sharon Porlier, "The Trustee Nature of Christian Art," *Journal for Christian Reconstruction* 1(1986): 11, 50.

3. Porlier, 58.

4. Wolfe, 16.

5. Juried exhibitions of this sort include: The annual Ecclesiastical Art Exhibit, by the Historic Trinity Lutheran Church, Detroit, Michigan; Arte Sagrado, by Concordia University at Austin; Sacred Arts, by The Billy Graham Center, Wheaton College; Works of Faith, by the First Presbyterian Church, Portland, Oregon; Cross Country, by Bethel College, Mishawaka, Indiana; National Christian Fine Arts Exhibit, by the First United Methodist Church, Farmington, New Mexico; Sacred Arts Show, by The Golden Isles Humanities Foundation, Brunswick, Georgia.   In addition, Christians in the Visual Arts (CIVA) sponsors juried exhibits in conjunction with both national and regional conferences.   Other local and regional Christian arts organizations sponsor local and regional juried exhibits.

Essay 17

Individualism

The Great artists, dying to self in their work, collaborate with their work, know it and are known by it as Adam knew Eve, and share in the mighty act of Creation.   That is our calling, the calling of all of us. But perhaps it is simplest for the artist (at work, at prayer) to understand, for nothing is created without this terrible entering into death.   It takes great faith, faith in the work if not conscious faith in God, for dying is fearful.   But without this death, nothing is born.   And if we die willingly, no matter how frightened we may be, we will be found, and born anew into life, and life more abundant.[1]

Madeleine L'Engle

Madeleine L'Engle writes that the artist must die to her work. Death prunes away biases, misconceptions, self-congratulation and many other personal failings that stand in the way of truth.   But how do we learn to die?   It is not the focus of many art classes or books on art.   There is no one way to do it; there are no rules about how to proceed.

A good first step is honesty.   If an artist can determine who he really is, what his real motives are (both good and bad) for making art, then it becomes easier to allow the false parts of our self-constructed persona to detach and break away.   Since art is integral to life within Christian community, this self-searching by the artist is necessary.

Artists need this honest approach because narcissism is not the domain of good artists.   They are in fact too busy looking at what they see before them, or at what they imagine in their mind, to be spending much time in front of the mirror.   An exceptional artist will be aware not only of what within his work is excellent, but also of its failings.   It is awareness that should make any of us humble, for the greater our awareness the greater is our understanding.   Our smallness and insignificance are magnified when we begin to understand.

Yet there are times when each of us finds ourselves holding on to something we have created, something into which we believe we have poured ourselves so fully that we are blind to the lies within it.   It is at this point, when our individual personality is at odds with the truth, that individualism becomes a negative.   For individualism *per se* is not a negative.

Each of us has been born and shaped into a unique human personality with our individualized physical, emotional and spiritual components.   It was God who made us individuals, and thus individualism is good.   And there are times when each individual must walk alone even when that is frightening or disconcerting.   Each of us has many decisions to make that nobody else can make for us without abusing our individual person-hood.

Healthy individualism is not a sin.   However, allowing individualism for its own sake to fill our minds will warp and disfigure us, make us less than human rather than fully human.   When individualism is disfigured by a self-absorption that makes us see and hear only what we desire to see and hear, then individualism has changed to narcissism.

Artists, and everyone else, are susceptible to the lures of individualism for its own sake.   Each of us has a head that can swell when our ears are filled with praises or our walls and drawers are filled with awards and trophies.   Perhaps narcissism is so often linked to the visual arts because the results of individualism for its own sake are so clear and obvious in the *fact* of a visual artwork.   It is much easier to skip bombastic or self-adulating pages in a book, or switch off the radio or television when personalized, self-serving hyperbole is broadcast, than it is to ignore a painting or sculpture that confronts us regularly.

However, narcissism is often extolled, for it allows the warrior artist to remain bold, belligerent and obsessed with his own "new" vision for art.   This is because artists of the twentieth century (and presumably the twenty-first century as well) coveted fame--a place in history.   Even though questing for fame is not new, ways to attain it have changed.

Instead of attempting to surpass what has gone before, we now seek to demolish the past.   For the Modern artist, the history of art is seen as a succession of clashes between styles or conceptual approaches.   The image chosen by many advocates of Modern art is the avant-garde.

This militant image implies destruction of the traditional, not reverence or even tolerance. And intolerance spawns narcissism.

However, before we ignore an artwork that another human has made, we must not summarily dismiss it as the product of a narcissist. Perhaps we need to ask questions of ourselves before we close our eyes to what may strike us as self-serving. Is the artist merely trying to get our attention? We are assaulted and confronted daily with a multitude of conflicting attempts to gain our attention. If an artist is too self-effacing, will anyone ever stop to look? Or is there something of value hidden behind the brash facade of an artwork that on first glance irritates or infuriates us?

God's methods have not always been subtle. Flooding the whole earth was probably considered by those drowned to have been a bit extreme. Elijah, when he confronted the 450 prophets of Baal, acted aggressively. How do we honestly know when we are being confrontational or aggressive that our reasons are good? How does the artist differentiate between justifiable assertiveness and self-aggrandizing or narcissistic pomposity within his own artwork? For in the midst of making an artwork, the artist feels called to serve that work, as L'Engle asserts.

Before the artist can discern whether his artwork represents a response dominated by self, or God, or some other purposes, some time may be needed for reflective contemplation. And is the means of presentation appropriate to and necessary for the communication this artwork holds?

Community, whether large or small, can become an antidote to self-serving individualism, but it can also snuff out the individuality that God has given each of us. So the artist should seek community response without holding it to be entirely reliable. In too many instances artists are pushed to the edges of a Christian community, or they are pushed out altogether.

Before the pious take aim at artists they perceive to be overly individualistic, they might wish to ponder their personal relationship with their target. Without a real and compassionate interpersonal relationship, criticism, especially negative criticism, will most often find a poor reception. How can an artist who is dismissed or ignored by a faith community be expected to receive admonition, when his faith community has chosen divorce rather than reconciliation?

If the faith community desires the right to admonish the overly individualistic approach of anyone, including artists, it should be willing to listen with an open mind. We seldom take to heart the criticism of a stranger, while we are more likely to listen to those with whom we are in relationship, with whom we have developed some degree of intimacy.

Much of what the Christian community has condemned has been condemned without any attempt at dialogue. The cliché of the "old West" often applies: "Shoot first, ask questions later!" This is not likely to encourage dialogue; it is however much easier to listen to a corpse than a living, breathing human who may see things differently than I do.

One such critic of contemporary art writes, "Man's noblest use of God's creation is art."[2] After the author extends his hand toward the artist with this compliment, he then goes on to write:

> Much of what attempts to pass as art today, for example, lacks the basic discipline, the command of the craft, necessary even to fall into the *category* of art. It cannot, therefore, bring man to God. Falsity cannot achieve truth. Today, what is inferior and even false parades as art under the guise of being "modern" art.[3]

The tone of another writer is even more caustic: "Like the architects of glass boxes, the daubers of random smears find themselves increasingly ignored."[4] These writers' negative comments indicate no serious desire to dialogue with contemporary artists. The dialogue is aborted with guns blazing before it can begin.

What has led to this dialogical deadlock? In truth we may wish to question a great deal of art from the twentieth century. Yet to verbally batter and assault those we disagree with is highly suspect as a Christian approach to dialogue. But then perhaps these writers did not desire dialogue. When we are right, why give those who are wrong a chance to converse?

Christian writers are not the only confrontational communicators. Christians as well as artists can become targets:

> Christian writing is propaganda, not literature, no matter what he [the author of the article that elicited this response] says. Its sole purpose is to perpetuate the hard-line Christian fanatic message of the Newt Gingrichs, the Ralph Reeds, the Karol Wojtylas, who control and manipulate tens of millions of people unwilling to think for themselves.[5]

Many holding opposing views have decided to throw the first stone; some of the stones are huge and abrasive, others are smoother and flung with greater accuracy.   The question should not be how can we shield ourselves from these attacks, but rather how can we restrain ourselves and keep ourselves from slinging our own stones before we think about the consequences?

There is a time for anger and the expression of anger.   There are times when we should defend ourselves.   Sometimes it may be best to ignore an attack, to refuse to rise to the bait and be drawn into the fray. Often, however, we cannot keep from being drawn into the struggle, for events overwhelm our reticence.   When this happens, we are faced with a hard choice.   Do we then become warriors drawing blood from each human target, seduced by the thrill and exhilaration of the battle itself?   Or do we seek to bring healing to the fallen, no matter which side they may have fought for?

Here the question of individualism really comes into play.   Do we believe that someone else's individualism is the problem?   Is it only when someone else intrudes into the space we call our own, that we then decide that individualism needs to be restricted?

Like most important issues, individualism is a two-way street. There will always be artists, critics, viewers, and politicians who will be condemned, usually by labeling them as fascists, fundamentalists, liberals, male chauvinists, feminists, philistines, libertines, homophobic, heteraphobic or something else intended to identify what makes either them, or what they stand for, seem despicable.

Those who would restrict individualism do not restrict themselves, and those who would rally to the cry of individual rights do not like it when some offended party expresses his or her individualism by slashing her artwork or the tires on his car.   All parties then don the mask of righteousness, so that each might each feel justified in pointing to the stupidity, cupidity, mendacity or monumental ignorance of those who would dare to take an alternative view.

Too often we speak because we feel compelled to justify ourselves or some theory or proposition we espouse.   We pay attention to the writer of Ecclesiastes only when he writes: "For everything there is a season . . . a time to speak" (Eccl 3: 1-7).   We so easily omit "a time to keep silence" (Eccl 3:7).

We Christians should not unthinkingly espouse the "straight and narrow path," for it allows access to so few.   A wide highway, one that allows many of us to walk side by side, would seem to be a preferable image, the King's highway.   On a narrow path only one can lead, all others must follow.   If we are the leaders traveling the narrow path, we cannot look at our followers or attend to their needs, for we fear the misstep that will cause all of us to tumble. If we follow another along the narrow path, we cannot see the way for ourselves, we view only another's backside. If each of us walks side by side with others, more eyes can search the way ahead, more ears can hear what may come from behind, and we can easily see and come to know each other as individuals.

But for the present however the avant-garde of the art world too often ignores the rest who follow behind. And the main body, which receives communications it cannot understand, is reluctant to budge an inch from where it is. In reality both the avant-garde and the main body restrict individualism; both demand their own version of politically correct conformity. On the one hand, individualism seems for the avant-garde often to be the ultimate value and for the main body it is the great fear. What can we hope for in this hostile environment? What role does individualism play?

Healthy individualism, as L'Engle suggests, occurs when we allow ourselves to be born anew, when we allow that which is not important to die. Dying is never a painless event. Much of this death is about letting go, about relinquishing the need to be in control of the process. As the unnecessary layers slide away, an artist becomes aware of her skills and gifts and what there is around her that is true or false; she can then begin to serve the truth. Allowing self to die so that truth may come to inhabit us is not easy, for many ideas and personalities and goals hold us in their grip. For the artist, as for everyone else, this dying is a continuing process. It is not something we complete and then move on to some new project, or new goal or new step. Dying to self is the step, the project, the goal; it is what each of us is called to do. And as we each press forward toward this death, we do not become less--we become more; we do not diminish--we expand; we do not become empty--we are filled.

But it is not actually our self that dies, only those parts of it that are not useful. As we discard what is no longer useful, we will find room for expanding what has value--we can grow. In this growth process we are filled with the truth that God makes available to anyone who would risk seeking it.

Dying to self is not to be in any way confused with suicide or the killing of individuality. For the sake of the work, the artist's self becomes devoted to the work and absorbed in the making of the work. Self is always present while the work is being made; the artist does not step out of his persona while in the act of making. Instead the self operates in obedience to the dictates of the artwork, observing--but not obtrusively--the process of making.   While making an artwork, the artist is not self-absorbed, rather she is work-absorbed--drawn into the making of the work.

Once the work is complete, the self reasserts self, demanding rest, demanding comfort, demanding food and many other legitimate necessities.   It is only when the primary underlying purpose of the artwork is to draw attention to the artist-maker that the art-making process becomes narcissistic.   But then the artist has not died to self in the process, death has only been feigned.   Giving up self for the sake of the artwork has never been and never will be perfected by any artist. But it is a worthy goal.

Unfortunately, our star system culture can only focus on the here and now.   The latest fad, the latest sensation is its focus.   Cultural hyperbole calls us into the battle, prods us to action, depending upon our narcissistic vulnerabilities to aid in the seduction.   In reality many narcissists are merely cannon fodder for the media.   Short-term adulation is given and then taken away without remorse.   It is a cruel and cynical war game.   It is a game that Christians should avoid, while at the same time crafting a better, alternative approach to vocation—to life.

Notes

1. Madeleine L'Engle, "Reflections on Faith and Art," *The Other Side* (December 1982): 12.

2. Richard J. Schuler, "Man, Art, God," *Triumph* (October 1970): 33.

3. Schuler, 34.

4. Otto Scott, "Modern Art Unmasked," *Journal for Christian Reconstruction* 1(1986): 75.

5. Nancy Wood, letter to the editor, *Poets and Writers* (March/April 1998): 4.

Essay 18

Education

Religion without artistic images is qualitatively impoverished; art without religion is in danger of triviality, superficiality, or subservience to commercial or political interests.[1]

Margaret R. Miles

Never once in my four years of undergraduate study as an art major at a large university was there any in-depth discussion of the why of art. Many classes and many hours were spent on the how of art. I learned how to use a variety of paint media, how to etch a zinc plate, how to print a lithograph from stone, how to draw the human figure, how to form a pot using the coil method and many other useful skills. I studied art history and got some understanding of how art and history were interrelated. My paintings and other pieces were discussed in critiques. But no professor ever discussed why it was important to make art. Maybe the question seemed too basic, or just unnecessary. I do not know.

While I was working on my M.F.A. at an institution with a high reputation in art, one professor questioned me about the myth behind my art. But he never made clear what he meant by myth. Only much later did I begin to think about what he may have meant. I believe he, like Rothko, Newman and other major artists, wanted to believe that art transcended its material substance, that there was some mythic dimension to it. Myth was the connection with the universal, myth took the artist beyond himself or herself and beyond the bounds of an individual culture, time or place. I may be wrong about this, but that is what I now think he wanted me to consider. Perhaps he was not able to clarify that link for himself, so in turn he could not clarify it for me either.

Mythic transcendence or some other type of spiritual transcendence was the goal of a number of twentieth century artists including Kandinsky, Chagall, Rouault, Brancusi, Newman and Rothko.   But this was not often at the center of what was discussed in the studio or art history classroom.

Myth was discussed in relation to Greek and Roman art or in terms of the Renaissance.   The spiritual was generally relegated to the Romanesque, Gothic and Baroque or other periods that were dominated by the Roman Catholic Church in Western Europe.   Why?

Often writers of art theory or history were either agnostics or atheists who did not value transcendence.   Others were Marxists or some other brand of materialists who had even less use for the concept of transcendence.   Possibly others were rebelling against or embarrassed by the institutional church and other traditional institutions.   Still others may have believed that myth and the spiritual were too ill defined for this age of science, where measurement and controlled observation are the demigods.   There may be many additional reasons for not discussing "Why should artists make art?"   Well, there was personal expression, but little attention was given even to this refuge of the narcissist.   Why?

The answer may well be that these professors, so skilled in art-making techniques and so knowledgeable in artistic style and composition, did not have an answer.   Art making did not need justification; making art is what humans have done for millennia. Whatever the answer, I was left wandering about as a student without much idea of why it was valuable to make art.   I did not think it was merely to fill up empty wall space, or to create commodities to feed the military industrial complex, or just to a search for a means of personal expression.

I think that in the past decade or two more effort is put into the why part of education for art majors.   I wish that I could say confidently that this was a genuine improvement over the years I spent studying art. But I can't.

The basis for much of the current why of art education focuses more often than not on one or another ideological perspective, with the potential to provide students with insight in to why art is a valuable thing to make.   Feminist art, environmental art, gay and lesbian art, Marxist art and other ideologically based approaches to art do provide a why: some set of beliefs, some theoretical or social perspective.   But none of these can match even my graduate professor's vague notion of myth.

A myth-based approach to art at least sought to interact with reality in terms of universal truths. Most ideological approaches to art seek rather to deflate myth, debunk religion (especially Western religions) and deny that there is anything that can be labeled "truth." I am not interested here in trying to determine why this is the case. Instead, I would like to propose some alternatives.

Educating artists is not an easy task. For one thing it is hard to be sure what any given artist at any given time might want or feel compelled to make. To educate an artist for any contingency is never possible. A major dilemma for any contemporary approach to education is the narrow-mindedness of the contemporary educational environment. Our educational culture places great value on pieces of paper: test scores, diplomas, certificates and transcripts. All these paper items are useful as historical documents. Test scores are records of testing events and somewhat predictive of future activity; diplomas and certificates are evidence that a course of study was completed. Transcripts provide historical information about courses taken and grades received. However, sad though it may be, none of these paper artifacts is particularly predictive of success within a particular discipline, and this is especially the case for vocations that require a high level of creativity.

I am not recommending that we throw out the educational system that generates these paper artifacts. I am suggesting that we place less value on them. Art schools and departments pay more attention to portfolios, and for good reason. A portfolio is more valuable both as a historical artifact and as a predictor of artistic potential. Yet most art schools and art departments are desperate to keep enrollment levels high. So most programs will take anyone with money and the desire to study art. Some students are allowed to remain in a program that might be better served by a probationary period, followed by a review and a decision about the readiness of the student for further study.

But bigger problems exist. One of the most absurd practices of contemporary education is the "one size fits most" approach. Instead of telling potential students your course of study can be completed in four years, art programs should say that the typical student completes the program in three to five years, but there is no set time sequence. The time it takes a to complete the course of study is dependent upon a particular student's ability. For each student comes with a different background and needs an individualized course of study to fit his or her particular needs, not to fit the needs of some nonexistent typical student (or the institution).

Along with this indeterminate length of study should come a more flexible curriculum. Some students may enter with a high level of skill in some areas while other students have minimal skills. Should both be forced to spend the same amount of time in a class designed to improve skills, understanding of methods and techniques or of compositional possibilities? From a housekeeping point of view the answer is yes. It is much simpler if all classes last a quarter or semester. It is much simpler to assume that all students will progress at a uniform rate of speed. If students do not perform well in such an environment, then it is clearly due to some inadequacy or laziness on their part. It would be more complicated and more difficult to create a system of education for artists that assumes that each individual is unique and develops at his or her individual rate. But this system would ultimately be less wasteful and more humane!

Mentors should play a much larger role in the education of artists. Some professors in some art programs may play the role of mentors, but there is no assurance that each student will be mentored. Each art student, from early on within the program, should have an experienced, practicing artist as a mentor. Mentors and students should meet once a week or every two weeks throughout the student's entire student career.

A mentor's role would not be primarily as technical advisor, helping the student to develop skills. Rather they could help students deal with the why questions of art. They could act as vocational models tying together those things that are introduced in art studio and art history classes in a way that fits the personality of a particular student. They could provide students with a perspective from which to view both their artistic successes and failures. The mentor, unlike advisors or professors, would be overseeing the education of the whole person.

Another failure of our contemporary educational system is the lack of opportunities to learn how to teach skills and methods and to share with other students the why of their own artistic output. One of the best ways to assure mastery of a particular skill or concept is to have the learner teach. Why not encourage and provide opportunities for students to teach each other? That would allow professors more time to be mentors, it would allow students to learn through teaching, and it could remove some of the anxiety for the student on the receiving end.

More genuine time ought to be spent in discussing how students want viewers to respond to the art they make and how viewers actually are responding to their work. Student peers can help in this process, and not just peers who are involved in the same studio discipline.

Another excellent way for students to learn is as apprentices. This old-fashioned approach to education had its problems, but also its values. Instead of studying with professors whom the student seldom sees working on actual artwork, the student can learn directly what is involved in making art, by being present when it happens. Learning the nuts and bolts of studio procedures often follows an apprenticeship model. Other disciplines have internships; art students should experience working in a professional studio environment.

One other advantage to the apprenticeship model is that it can dispel some of the Romantic notions about creative activity. Students will learn that making art is not some mysterious process; rather it is like any other activity that involves making a product. A student will also get a better idea of what it is like to be a professional artist, and more importantly, whether being an artist is the right vocation to prepare for.

What I am proposing is missing from most institutions of higher education, which are forced to fit learning into set time blocks and set methods of evaluation. Too much teacher effort is now spent in determining grades, and too much student effort is focused on receiving a desired grade rather than on learning what can be learned.

There are risks to any approach to education one might take. However, the current approach to educating often functions more like a straitjacket for both professors and students when it should be providing opportunities and flexibility.

Let's try mentors, flexible learning periods, and apprenticeships; they may provide the freedom to explore artistic possibilities while providing a real anchor, not merely a hypothetical one. Apprenticeships focus on the reality of making a product, flexible learning periods treat students as individual humans, and mentors can provide and encourage the freedom to think and feel and explore. And in the end, students will gain a better image than I could as a student of why they are seeking to become artists and why they wish to make art.

Notes

1. Margaret R. Miles, *Images as Insight* (Boston: Beacon Press, 1985), 151.

Essay 19

Authenticity

[B]ut the lie of Hoffmann's picture is that the artist has been insensitive to Christ's agony and lacks insight into the meaning of the event. Hoffmann says nothing significant. He renders only appearances.[1]

Nancy Snooks

We are called, as Christians, to be filled with loving-kindness. However, at the same time we are called to honor truth. How does one recognize the authentic? How does one detect the inauthentic? Such discernment is not simple. Though it may be easy to render judgment about a particular artwork, it is not easy to render justice. Each of us brings so much baggage with us to the court of authenticity that we forget about the biases, blind spots and hatreds that affect our judgments.

How can the artist who may abhor Hoffman's overt sentimentality and the believer who finds comfort in Hoffman's images reconcile their conflicting views? The burden for reconciliation is not to be dumped soley upon the conscientious believer who wishes to be comforted. Are comfortable images wrong *per se*? Matisse's answer was no. He wanted his art to be "something like a good armchair in which to rest from physical fatigue."[2] If seeking comfort within an artwork is valid, then what do we do about Hoffman, and other artists, who make use of sentimental seductions? Is anyone to blame for smoothing over the rough-textured surface of truth with sentimentality?

Who benefits from providing believers with sentimental images? "Who profits from them?" is an even better question. Christian publishing houses and Christian businesses can easily sell these works, for many buyers want and need to be comforted. All of us suffer from loss or illness and the ravages of contemporary life. And we want to be comforted, we want to have our feet washed, we want to feel the perfumed ointment rubbed into our weary muscles.

Unfortunately some Christian publishers and businesses provide us the visual equivalent of a chemically sanitized towelet instead. How can artists and others who honor truth in art replace the counterfeit image and bring about change? Here again, there is no simple answer. One route would be to ridicule counterfeit images and the stupidity of anyone who would prefer them to the real thing. A second route, clearly preferable, would be to provide a more authentic alternative so that discerning buyers could make the right choice. But how do we create the necessary discernment so that buyers and viewers will choose the authentic?

Isn't that the central question every individual struggles with daily? The question of authenticity is the question of choosing life (what is authentic and enhances life) over death (what is inauthentic and does not enhance life). And you an I, if we are honest, know that we do not always choose life. Many of our decisions, both large and small, have not been for life.

If artists and art critics want believers to choose life, or the authentic, then they must engage in a dialogue with believers, both through their work and through their words. In successful dialogue artists and critics model themselves on Christ. Since Christ could both wash the feet of his disciples and condemn the hypocrisy of the Pharisees, his model allows for a wide range of interactions. In choosing which approach to take, the artist or critic will need to examine his or her own ability to discern the appropriate (life-affirming) style and form and content.

When it comes to sentimental art, like that of Hoffman, the determination of authenticity versus inauthenticity is not overwhelmingly difficult. Like Frank and Dorothy Getlein, we can see that "the work is a lie."[3] Hoffman's Christ is not at all like the Christ we have learned to know from the Bible. His Christ has just come from the beauty salon. He is not a Christ capable of sweating blood or struggling with the extreme anguish of the crucifixion that confronts him.

When we look at other works of art, the mix of truth and untruth may make the determination of authenticity more difficult. Snooks, when evaluating Salvador Dali's *Sacrament of the Last Supper*, comes to the conclusion that "there is some incongruity in this picture: a lack of integrity and integration."[4] Frank Gaebelein objects to this painting because of Dali's "blond Christ on a cross suspended between heaven and earth."[5] Dali, in Gaebelein's view, has neglected truth. On the other hand Doug Adams has found this same painting to provide understanding about the relationship between Christ and communion. For Adams the overlapping of images "helps us to remember the whole Biblical story rather than just one episode."[6] And Maurice B. McNamee writes of another Dali painting, *The Christ of St. John of the Cross*:

> It reaches back to the historical moment of the crucifixion; it comes forward to the church in time which perpetuates the fruits of the redemptive death of Christ, and makes the significance of that death contemporary to any viewer.[7]

What do we do when some Christians say that a Dali painting lacks integrity and lacks truth while other Christians find Dali's paintings significant to their Christian life?

We can find other examples of disagreement about the authenticity of particular art works and on the art of particular artists. Paintings by Jackson Pollock brings both supporters and detractors to the pages of periodicals. David Jasper sees Pollock's *Cathedral* as "in a sense, deeply sacramental as a mystical space between the finite and the infinite, its quality of the absolute removes it from the biblical and theological narratives of great churches."[8] On the other hand Calvin Seerveld characterizes Pollock's paintings as filled with "a deadly serious, violent, gigantic histrionics in the technique of raw paint."[9]

While one critic finds Pollock's painting to be deeply sacramental, the other finds his paintings to be histrionic. What has led to such opposite reactions and interpretations? No doubt probing would lead us to somewhat divergent theological perspectives, divergent personalities with divergent sensibilities. Yet both critics have a concern for both art and Christianity. Seerveld is concerned with a long historical tradition (a tradition that Pollock turns his back on) that reveres rationality, while Jasper is captivated by mysticism and finds Pollock's *Cathedral* works an entry point for mystical contemplation. Who is right? Who is wrong? Are both men partly right and partly wrong, or does what they find in Pollock's paintings merely reflect personal predisposition and bias?

I think that Seerveld's concern for rationality is a legitimate concern. Some contemporary artists clearly have no respect for rationality or tradition. They seek their place in history through notoriety. I also value Jasper's openness to mystical experiences, an openness that places values on what cannot be fully understood.

I know that sometimes I react positively to artworks because I am impressed with what is communicated (intellectually, spiritually and/or emotionally) and how it is communicated.   This may be because somehow who I am intellectually, spiritually and/or emotionally is in sync with what is expressed.   I also know that I react negatively to art works because they grate upon me aesthetically, or because I disagree with them conceptually, or because they threaten me emotionally.

But are my reactions integral to the artwork alone, or are they equally dependent upon my fallen and imperfect humanness? Whatever I see and how I apprehend what I see in an artwork is relational.   I react negatively or positively depending upon the emotional, spiritual and intellectual constructs I have formulated. When an artwork does not challenge my construct, then it is acceptable. (Of course our construct may be that artworks should challenge our construct, but that does not alter the issue.)   When an artwork does challenge my construct, then it is unacceptable.   But I know my constructs are fallible because I have changed my mind, sometimes more than once in relation to my judgment of a particular artwork.   I change my mind because I am in dialogue with the various communities of which I am a part, the art community, the Christian community and other communities.

It is through dialogue that we come to know where we stand.   And it is good to stand somewhere rather than merely float (take no position). We can always move to another position should the current standing point no longer remain viable.   When I look back at the divergent places that I have stood, it sometimes looks as though I were hopping, rather than following some clear path.   What's more important, however, is that I see that my position has changed--often.   And actually these changes show that I have not yet become a fossil; rather they give evidence that I am alive and growing.

So as we dialogue, I hope that we can overlay with tolerance our discussions about art and faith.   I hope that each of us will listen and respond openly to input, to alternative experiences and points of view, and that we can each continue to grow.   This openness is not merely the responsibility of the artist or critic, it is also the responsibility of the viewer, the receiver of the artwork, as well.

Notes

1. Nancy Snooks, "Authenticity and Inauthenticity in Modern Religious Art," *Communio* (Winter 1974): 395.   The painting Snooks refers to is Heinrich Hoffmann's *Christ in the Garden of Gethsemane.*

2. Henri Matisse, "Notes of a Painter," *Theories of Modern Art*, ed. by. Herschel B. Chipp (Berkeley: University of California Press, 1968), 135.

3. Frank and Dorothy Getlein, *Christianity in Modern Art* (Milwaukee: The Bruce Publishing Company, 1961), 27.

4. Snooks, 396.

5. Frank E. Gaebelein, "The Creator and Creativity," *Christianity Today* (October 5, 1984): 36.

6. Doug Adams, "Becoming the Body of Christ in Resurrected Communion," *Church Teachers* (March-May, 1989): 178.

7. Maurice B. McNamee, "The Image of Christ in Modern Art," *Communio* (Winter 1974): 422.

8. David Jasper, "Theology and American Abstract Expressionism," *ARTS: The Arts in Religious and Theological Studies* 7(1995): 17.

9. Calvin Seerveld, "Can Art Survive the Secular Onslaught?" *Christianity Today* (July 17, 1981): 72.

Essay 20

Being

In solitude we can listen to the voice of him who spoke to us before we could speak a word, who healed us before we could make any gesture to help, who set us free long before we could free others, and who loved us long before we could give love to anyone. It is in this solitude that we discover that being is more important than having, and that we are worth more than the result of our efforts. In solitude we discover that our life is not a possession to be defended, but a gift to be shared.[1]

Henri J. M. Nouwen

Each of us is. Each life is filled with being-ness. We are, we think, we experience, we do; all of this is part of and imparts our being-ness. There is no split between doing and being; doing is a part of being--an active part. For the artist the making of art is an essential part of her being. For the receiver of art receptivity is an essential part of his being. Being in its wholeness is made up of thinking, praying, feeling, composing, making, proposing, accepting, receiving and responding. Wholeness of being depends upon both receiving and giving. The absence of either receiving or giving is part of brokenness. In this fallen world all of us are broken. We have, in our fallenness, forgotten how to be unbroken receivers and unbroken givers. Prayer and meditation and art, if entered into with a desire for knowing, can bring healing.

Art itself, unlike each of us, does not have being. Being depends upon the individual's awareness of being. Artworks can however evoke or lead or direct us into the presence of another's being. In true artworks lives the potentiality of introduction. Through such artworks, if we open ourselves to them, we are introduced to another. This other may be the artist-maker of the artwork or it may be that to whom the

artist-maker directs our attention.   The artist-maker forms a new entity
that may have a potentially profound impact upon our being.

The artist may be in some ways like John the Baptist: she directs our
vision towards that which is truly Holy--her artwork may be "the voice
of one crying in the wilderness: 'Prepare the way of the Lord'" (Mt
3:3).   Even so, how do we then come to grips with the other that
resides within this new artistic entity?   "Face to face," as George
Steiner suggests, "the presence of the offered meaning which we call
text (or a painting or a symphony), we seek to hear its language.   As
we would that of the elect stranger coming towards us."[2] Each artwork
we address is like this stranger of unknown character and content.
Each of us can choose to welcome or ignore this stranger.   Whatever
we choose, risk is inherent in our choice.   The artist, or the presence to
which the artist directs us, may overwhelm us, change us in ways
beyond prediction.

Being reserved is no disgrace.   Wearing the self-protective garments
of reticence and reserve reflects wisdom.   However, if we choose to
interact with the artwork, "the movement towards reception and
apprehension does embody an initial, fundamental act of trust."[3] Within
God's creation there are times when we are called to risk the anxiety
and discomfort of trust.   Each of us can remember when we trusted
rightly and were repaid with acceptance and respect.   We can also
remember times when our trust was harshly abused and we were made
to feel less than fully human.   However, if we are not to remain
confined or imprisoned by our own timidity, we would do well to make
the effort to befriend artworks that seek to engage our being.   If we
choose confinement over the risk of introduction, then we may
condemn ourselves to the desolation of loneliness, and beyond that we
risk atrophying our being.

This does not mean that we should open ourselves to every artistic
stranger that comes our way.   Not all artistic strangers, any more than
all human strangers, are to be trusted.   We must remain watchful and
aware.   Do the engaging qualities that originally attracted our attention
to this previously unknown painting or sculpture or tapestry bring us
closer to a presence that is good and honest or hide some moral or
emotional defect?   Good and honest works engage us with respect,
they treat us humanely--such artworks may soothe us in our suffering
or confront us with the lies we tell ourselves.

Perhaps we should allow very few artworks to peel away our mask
of polite reserve, as did the woman at the well when she allowed Christ
to disarmingly dissolve her public face.   Some artworks that direct us

to Christ may work that kind of miracle of truth upon each of us, while others will not engage us beyond the polite pleasantries of socially accepted banter.

The location of our being, the emotional, intellectual and spiritual exigencies that have placed their varied demands upon our being, may predispose us not to befriend a new artwork. Our path up to the present moment has woven our emotional dispositions, shaped our intellects and framed our spiritual outlook. How we react to a new artwork tells us as much about our self as it does about what the artwork presents. It is easier sometimes to interact with those statues or engravings that we have previously befriended. There is no reason to feel guilty for this preference for the known. For as we reengage the known artwork, if it has any depth, it too will continue to surprise us with revelation. In truth, we find that if we reengage the known with true receptivity and invitation, and with an awareness of the present state of our being, that we will come away from this dialogue or encounter with new and deeper understanding.

As the artist considers the meaning, the presence that her artwork evokes, it may remind her of the seriousness of her vocation. She will want to be acutely aware of and understand as fully as possible the potential impact of her artworks--those strangers she sends into the world. Beyond self-awareness, which is difficult enough--there is a need for responsibility. Artists of artworks that invade, sadistically overwhelm, or wreak havoc upon the unwitting who encounter them with receptivity, cannot innocently deny responsibility. An artwork has the potential to attack us at the core of our personhood, to change how we think or what we believe, to reduce us to uncontrolled weeping.

Yet this call to accountability is in no way meant to silence the artist. For the artist who timidly keeps himself from speaking into being the drawings or assemblages or relief prints that may lead another into intimate and healing encounter with God or God's creation or Christ's humanity will also be held accountable. The artist who is alive to the reality and nature of his own being can make works that will be good and honest friends--artworks--to those who would befriend them. It is this alive-ness to our own being that is essential to all those who would self-label themselves Christian, artists or otherwise. It is when the artist is not alive to his own being that he succumbs to unawareness and makes kitsch, that inoffensive but non-nourishing artistic substitute.

Kitsch is absence of presence; it is something made by a stifled or unaware person--and by kitsch, I mean an image or form that has been reduced by its maker to visual cliché.   Kitsch can introduce us to nothing that is life transforming.   For its maker put no life into it! Kitsch unlike real art leads nowhere.   It is the yes-man of the art world; the preferred (but non-nutritional) food of the narcissist--the receiver that wishes only a mirror that reflects his own answer.

If the artist is true to her being, she will not make kitsch.   Being true to the self that God has gifted you with propels you towards creating artworks that will engage the viewer either with the reality of your own being, or with the reality of other beings--with presence.

Since God infuses the artist-maker with the gift of making art, what the artist makes is not wholly of his making.   God does not shape the artist into a conduit or transmitting device.   But God's personality is present in the artist-maker, as the artist is present in what he makes. Each artwork made by the artist who is open to God contains evidences or murmurs or whispers spoken by the hands of God.   The very freedom to make art that God's gifting imparts itself reflects God's image from within the artist.

Each artist, depending on his or her depth of awareness, is cognizant of this echo of God's voice in the forms envisioned and crafted within the freedom of artistic creation.   God's role is that of the Basso Continuo for all creation: artists building on the solidity of this endless and continuing foundation form melodies and harmonies as imaginative as the personality and giftedness of the artist allows.   God, with unimaginable generosity, allows the artist to hold the brush or pen or chisel and to speak visual form into the world.   It is the artist who ignores or is unaware of God's baseline or foundation who creates disharmonies that weigh down and diminish those who open themselves up, too carelessly, to any artistic stranger who might approach them wearing a mask that hides the discord that dwells within.

On the other hand, when the artist works with the assurance of the undergirding of God's through bass, she can embrace the freedom of the infinite possibility of both melody and harmony--she can dance her visual forms forth with intuitive (knowing) grace.   Without awareness of God's through bass, the artist is destined to become imprisoned within the confines of some fashionable or unfashionable aesthetic ideology, and thus utterly dependent upon the determination and verbal facility of its adherents.   As long as the adherents of a particular fashionable style paint or sculpt, and critics provide justification, the merely fashionable will survive.   But once the artist's hands stop making and the critics stop asserting, the merely fashionable in art ceases to wear its mask of presence.

When artists make artworks that are not the willing or unwilling slaves to fashion or critical dogma, viewers receive real nourishment. The receiving viewer-participant, when some aesthetic ideology is not the sole determiner of visual forms, can catch and share the grace-filled freedom within which the artist works. When the being of the artist is freed to make, then the viewer-participant is also enfranchised and can participate in this freedom, to dialogue, to dance, to participate in the thoughts, feelings and movements of the artwork. This duet or trio between maker and participant is not merely intellectual. It can be much more intimate than that. Individual beings, through art, can be brought together in an emotionally, intellectually and spiritually embodied communion that transcends time and place. The reality of that communion is as substantial as anything found in the material actuality we see or touch or feel.

Notes

1. Henri J. M. Nouwen, *Out of Solitude* (Notre Dame, Indiana: Ave Maria Press, 1974), 22.
2. George Steiner, *Real Presences* (Chicago: University of Chicago Press, 1989), 156.
3. Steiner, 156.

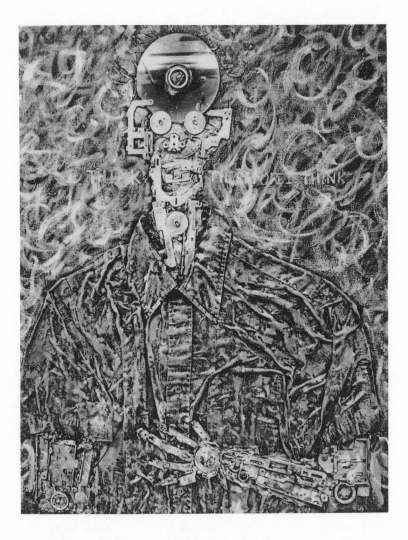

Douglas Campbell, *Homo Silicon*, acrylics and computer parts on canvas,
30"x24.25", 2000

Homo Silicon

As we enter a new millennium, many are choosing faith in technology over faith in God. They have come to believe humankind is coming closer to understanding the codes carried by human genes. Or they believe we can engineer a better biological environment so that our crops will be more pest and disease resistant. Or they believe our lives will be continually made better by further technological developments in computer science.

It is possible that human life may continually be enhanced by technology. But it will not solve our most difficult problems. It will not improve human interactions and communal relationships. It will not end divorce or child abuse, or bring about peace between long-time enemies. We endanger our world and ourselves when we put our faith in technological salvation.

Technology brings the bad with the good. With computers communications can take place almost instantaneously, but email makes it just as quick and easy to insult or commend, spread a rumor or share love. Technology can change the means, but it seldom changes substance. It can help physicians make our bodies look better, but it has not made us better at taking care of our bodies. We are a nation spending millions on exercise equipment and exercise paraphernalia and even more on weight control and reduction. Technology may make life easier, but not necessarily better.

Art will not always make our lives easier or better, but it may help us remain more human and humane. Art can help us to battle against becoming *Homo Silicon,* a being that amasses data, calculates, provides statistical profiles, controls functions and allows for instantaneous "communication."

Because art focuses on sensations and emotions as well as ideas and concepts, art, though it is not salvation, can be a means of pointing us in the right direction.   Art forces on us, and not always conveniently, body awareness.   Textures, colors and shapes enter our bodies through sight and touch and movement, cause us to have bodily reactions--chills, warmth, perspiration--that remind us that we are not disembodied minds.   Humans need to learn to balance mind and body, not ignoring either to the detriment of the other.

Our minds and bodies may be stimulated by virtual reality, but virtual reality is still no more than an elaborate hoax, a bundle of tricks or a shell game.   At least some of the time our minds and bodies need the truth that can be found in real objects, images that don't fade from a screen with the flick of a switch.   Virtual reality and electronic images on a screen are intriguing and seductive. Even though they may be productive for some therapies or simulations they are much like aspartame--no food value and its own deleterious side effects.   And often technology provides an aspartame equivalent that gives us nothing and leaves an unpleasant aftertaste.   But art may feed our minds, spirits and bodies, in part because of art's holistic nature that speaks to our intellects, souls and emotions.

Purveyors of technology, at least as currently envisioned and promoted, seek to reduce real work (usually meaning unpleasant physical activities), seek to reduce the number of tasks needing human input, and seek to interpose technology into our culture in a way that weakens rather than enhances interpersonal contact.   But art engages humans directly through their senses.   The making of art is a physical activity, not a virtual or theoretical activity.   Art is labor intensive, it is a squandering of time if viewed from any utilitarian perspective.   And last but not least, art seeks to engage the viewer in discussion either with the artist-maker or with others who participate in the art process by viewing, touching and moving about interactively with art objects. Often such interaction with an artwork leads to discussion or the making of other art objects that function as confirmation or counterproposals.

Christianity, which centers on a God who is incarnated in human form, is uniquely privileged.   For Christians, and therefore for artists who are Christians, spirit and body are both honored.   For Christians, God is not just a disembodied spirit who has no understanding of what it is like to live a brief span within a body that is both wonderful and fragile.   God too knows from direct experience what it is like to touch and be touched.   God knows the joys of color and light and texture, not merely as divine constructs spoken forth in creation, but from personal, sensual experience.   God did not give us a virtual world; instead God gave us this real world with artists and their many gifts so that we could celebrate together his creation and our humanness within that creation.

Bibliography

Books

Apostolos-Cappadona, Diane, ed. *Art, Creativity and the Sacred: An Anthology in Religion and Art.* New York: Crossroad, 1984.

Breslin, James E.B. *Mark Rothko: A Biography.* Chicago: Univ. of Chicago Press, 1993.

Bustard, Ned, ed. *It Was Good: Making Art to the Glory of God.* Baltimore: Square Halo Books, 2000.

Chipp, Herschel B., ed. *Theories of Modern Art: A Sourcebook by Artists and Critics.* Berkeley: Univ. California Press, 1968.

Danto, Arthur. *Embodied Meanings: Critical Essays and Aesthetic Meditations.* New York: Farrar Straus Giroux, 1994.

Davies, Horton, and Hugh Davies. *Sacred Art in a Secular Century.* Collegeville, Minnesota: The Liturgical Press, 1978.

Dickie, George, and Richard Sclafani, eds. *Aesthetics: A Critical Anthology.* New York: St. Martin's Press, 1977.

Dillenberger, Jane Daggett. *The Religious Art of Andy Warhol.* New York: Continuum, 1998.

Getlein, Frank, and Dorothy Getlein. *Christianity in Modern Art.* Milwaukie: The Bruce Publishing Company, 1961.

Greenberg, Clement. *Art and Culture: Critical Essays.* Boston: Beacon Press, 1961.

Harries, Richard. *Art and the Beauty of God: A Christian Understanding.* London: Mowbray, 1993.

Kung, Hans. *Art and the Question of Meaning.* Translated by Edward Quinn. New York: Crossroad, 1981.

Laeuchli, Samuel. *Religion and Art in Conflict: Introduction to a Cross-Disciplinary Task.* Philadelphia: Fortress Press, 1980.

Maritain, Jacques. *Art and Scholasticism.* Translated by J. F. Scanlan. New York: Scribner, 1954.

Merton, Thomas. *No Man Is an Island.* New York: Harcourt Brace Jovanovich, 1955.

Miles, Margaret R. *Images as Insight.* Boston: Beacon Press, 1985.

Nouwen, Henri J. M. *Out of Solitude.* Notre Dame, Indiana: Ave Maria Press, 1974.

Rookmaaker, H. R. *Modern Art and the Death of Culture.* Downers Grove, Ill.: InterVarsity Press, 1978.

Schaeffer, Francis A. *Art and the Bible: Two Essays.* Downers Grove, Ill.: InterVarsity Press, 1973.

Scott, Steve. *Like a House on Fire: Renewal of the Arts in Postmodern Culture.* Chicago: Cornerstone Press Chicago, 1997.

Seerveld, Calvin G. *Rainbows for a Fallen World.* Toronto: Tuppence Press, 1980.

Steiner, George. *Real Presences.* Chicago: Univ. of Chicago Press, 1989.

Stiles, Kristine, and Peter Selz, eds. *Theories and Documents of Contemporary Art: A Sourcebook of Artists' Writings.* Berkeley: Univ. California Press, 1966.

Stolorow, Robert D., Bernard Bandshaft, and George E. Atwood. *Psychoanalytic Treatment: An Intersubjective Approach.* Hillsdale N.J.: The Analytic Press, 1987.

Tillich, Paul. *On Art and Architecture.* Ed. by John Dillenburger. Translated by Robert P. Scharlman. New York: Crossroad, 1987.

Veith, Gene Edward. *Postmodern Times: A Christian Guide to Contemporary Thought and Culture.* Wheaton, Ill.: Crossway Books, 1994.

Wolfe, Gregory. *Sacred Passion: The Art of William Schikel.* Notre Dame, Indiana: Univ. of Notre Dame Press, 1998.

Woltersdorf, Nicholas. *Art in Action.* Grand Rapids, Mich.: William B. Eerdmans Publishing Company, 1980.

Articles

Adams, Doug. "Becoming the Body of Christ in Resurrected Communion." *Church Teachers* (March-May 1989): 178-181.

Allen, Ronald B. "The Road to Distinction." *Discipleship Journal* (1987): 31-33.

Apostolos-Cappadona, Diane. "Dreams and Visions: Religious Symbols and Contemporary Culture." *Religion and Intellectual Life* (Spring 1984): 95-109.

Bazin, Ken. "Reclaiming the Arts." *ACTION* (Summer 1977): 12-15.

Campbell, Douglas G. "The Role of Art." *Voices in the Wilderness* (March/April 1988): 10-12.

Dillenberger, John. "Religion and the Sensibilities of the Artist." *Faith and Form* (Autumn 1978): 12-13, 21-27.

Gaebelein, Frank E. "The Creator and Creativity." *Christianity Today* (October 5, 1984): 33-38.

Hall, Linda. "Tsimsian Witness." *Christian Life* (July 1978): 45-46.

Henry, Patrick. "Religion and Art: The Uneasy Alliance." *Religion in Life* (Winter 1980): 448-460.

Jasper, David. "Theology and American Abstract Expressionism." *ARTS: The Arts in Religious and Theological Studies* 7(1995): 21-25.

Jenson, Robert W. "Beauty." *Dialog* (Fall 1986): 250-259.

L'Engle, Madeleine. "Listening to the Story." Interview by Dee Dee Risher. *The Other Side* (Mar.-Apr. 1998): 36-39.

------. "Reflections on Faith and Art." *The Other Side* (December 1982): 10-12.

McGovern, Robert M. "A Re-emergence of Religious Art in the Seventies." *Dimension* (Summer 1974): 87-90.

McNamee, Maurice B. "The Image of Christ in Modern Art." *Communio* (Winter 1974): 413-425.

Nes, Solrunn. "In the Image of God: An Interview with Solrunn Nes." *Areopagus* (Pentecost 1991): 32-35.

Parker, Peggy. "A Journey of Discovery." *ARTS:The Arts in Religious and Theological Studies* (Summer 1977): 4-8.

Pattison, George. "Art and Apologetics." *Modern Churchman* 32 (1991): 24-30.

Porlier, Sharon. "The Trustee Nature of Christian Art." *Journal of Christian Reconstruction* 1(1986): 46-62.

Rochelle, Jay C. "Proclamation and Vision." *Dialog* (Spring 1981): 93-95.

Ross, Susan A. "The Aesthetic and the Sacramental." *Worship* (January 1985): 2-17.

Saliers, Don E. "Beauty and Holiness Revisited: Some Relations Between Aesthetics and Theology." *Worship* (May 1974): 278-293.

Schuler, Richard J. "Man, Art, God." *Triumph* (October 1970): 33-35.

Scott, Otto. "Modern Art Unmasked." *Journal for Christian Reconstruction* 1(1986): 73-76.

Seerveld, Calvin G. "Can Art Survive the Secular Onslaught." *Christianity Today* (July 17, 1981):71-71,74-75.

------. "Relating Christianity to the Arts." *Christianity Today* (Novermber 7, 1980): 48-49.

Snooks, Nancy. "Authenticity and Inauthenticity in Modern Religious Art." *Communio* (Winter 1974): 394-412.

Stare, Sharlyn Welker. "Reclaiming the Reflections of the Creator." *Key to Christian Education* (Winter 1986): 1-3.

Walker, Ken. "The Sculpture that Speaks." *Charisma* (October 1994): 54-60.

Wolfe, Gregory. "Art, Faith, and the Stewardship of Culture." *Regeneration Quarterly* (Spring 1996): 16-18.

Wood, Nancy. Letter to the editor. *Poets and Writers* (March/April 1998): 4.

Index